BREAK
THESE RULES

BREAK
THESE RULES

35 YA Authors on Speaking Up,
Standing Out, and Being Yourself

EDITED BY LUKE REYNOLDS

CHICAGO
REVIEW
PRESS

"Be a Jock *or* a Nerd. Pick a Side. We're at War." Copyright © 2013 by Josh Berk; "Shhhhh" Copyright © 2013 by A. S. King; "It's Better to Be Safe Than Sorry" Copyright © 2013 by Matthew Quick; "Listening Is a Waste of Time" Copyright © 2013 by Olugbemisola Rhuday-Perkovich; "Never Be Alone" Copyright © 2013 by Francisco X. Stork; "Don't Tell" Copyright © 2013 by Neesha Meminger; "Don't Quit" Copyright © 2013 by Carl Deuker; "Be Clean!" Copyright © 2013 by Gary D. Schmidt; "Never Talk About Religion" Copyright © 2013 by Sara Zarr; "Follow the Money, Not Your Heart" Copyright © 2013 by Lisa Schroeder; "Look Like a Magazine Cover" Copyright © 2013 by Sayantani DasGupta; "Don't Tell Lies" Copyright © 2013 by Leslie Connor; "Pretend the Dark Stuff Isn't True" Copyright © 2013 by Carol Lynch Williams; "Don't Daydream" Copyright © 2013 by Wendy Mass; "Go to College After High School" Copyright © 2013 by Chris Barton; "Be Cool" Copyright © 2013 by Kathryn Erskine; "See Yourself Through the Eyes of Others" Copyright © 2013 by Jennifer Reynolds; "Speak Up!" Copyright © 2013 by Mike Jung; "Always Sit in Your Assigned Seat . . ." Copyright © 2013 by Lyn Miller-Lachmann; "Be Normal" Copyright © 2013 by Jennifer A. Nielsen; "Don't Clash with the Crowd" Copyright © 2013 by Anna Staniszewski; "Compare Yourself to Others" Copyright © 2013 by Luke Reynolds; "Be Productive" Copyright © 2013 by Jennifer Ziegler; "Always Know Where You're Going" Copyright © 2013 by Brian Yansky; "Don't Get Fat" Copyright © 2013 by Lisa Burstein; "Two Is Better than One" Copyright © 2013 by Natalie Dias Lorenzi; "Follow the Directions" Copyright © 2013 by Tamara Ellis Smith; "Grow Up. Be Serious." Copyright © 2013 by Tara Lazar; "Boys Don't Cry" Copyright © 2013 by Chris Lynch; "The Boy/Girl Rule" Copyright © 2013 by Pat Schmatz; "Be a Man" Copyright © 2013 by Rob Buyea; "Dress Appropriately" Copyright © 2013 by Margo Rabb; "There Are Firm Rules in Life" Copyright © 2013 by Thanhha Lai; "Don't Let the New World Change You" Copyright © 2013 by Mitali Bose Perkins; "Me First" Copyright © 2013 by Lynda Mullaly Hunt
Published by Chicago Review Press, Incorporated
814 North Franklin Street • Chicago, Illinois 60610

Cover & interior design: Andrew J. Brozyna

Library of Congress
Cataloging-in-Publication Data
Break these rules : 35 YA authors on speaking up, standing out, and being yourself / edited by Luke Reynolds.

pages cm

Audience: Grade 9 to 12.

ISBN 978-1-61374-784-1 (trade paper)

1. Teenagers--Conduct of life--Juvenile literature. 2. Self-realization--Juvenile literature. 3. Individuality--Juvenile literature. I. Reynolds, Luke, 1980-

BJ1661.B725 2013

155.5'19--dc23

2013011885

Printed in the United States of America
5 4 3 2 1

For the future rule breakers and status quo shakers. (For you.)

CONTENTS

INTRODUCTION: 35 WAYS TO BE WHO YOU REALLY ARE 1

BE A JOCK *OR* A NERD. PICK A SIDE. WE'RE AT WAR. 5
    JOSH BERK

SHHHHH 9
    A. S. KING

IT'S BETTER TO BE SAFE THAN SORRY 13
    MATTHEW QUICK

LISTENING IS A WASTE OF TIME 23
    OLUGBEMISOLA RHUDAY-PERKOVICH

NEVER BE ALONE 29
    FRANCISCO X. STORK

DON'T TELL 33
    NEESHA MEMINGER

DON'T QUIT 39
    CARL DEUKER

BE CLEAN! 41
    GARY D. SCHMIDT

NEVER TALK ABOUT RELIGION 51
    SARA ZARR

FOLLOW THE MONEY, NOT YOUR HEART 55
    LISA SCHROEDER

LOOK LIKE A MAGAZINE COVER 59
    SAYANTANI DASGUPTA

DON'T TELL LIES 67
LESLIE CONNOR

PRETEND THE DARK STUFF ISN'T TRUE 73
CAROL LYNCH WILLIAMS

DON'T DAYDREAM 79
WENDY MASS

GO TO COLLEGE AFTER HIGH SCHOOL 85
CHRIS BARTON

BE COOL 89
KATHRYN ERSKINE

SEE YOURSELF THROUGH THE EYES OF OTHERS 95
JENNIFER REYNOLDS

SPEAK UP! 101
MIKE JUNG

ALWAYS SIT IN YOUR ASSIGNED SEAT... 105
LYN MILLER-LACHMANN

BE NORMAL 111
JENNIFER A. NIELSEN

DON'T CLASH WITH THE CROWD 115
ANNA STANISZEWSKI

COMPARE YOURSELF TO OTHERS 119
LUKE REYNOLDS

BE PRODUCTIVE 125
JENNIFER ZIEGLER

ALWAYS KNOW WHERE YOU'RE GOING 131
BRIAN YANSKY

DON'T GET FAT 137
LISA BURSTEIN

TWO IS BETTER THAN ONE 143
NATALIE DIAS LORENZI

FOLLOW THE DIRECTIONS 149
TAMARA ELLIS SMITH

GROW UP. BE SERIOUS. 157
TARA LAZAR

BOYS DON'T CRY 161
CHRIS LYNCH

THE BOY/GIRL RULE 165
PAT SCHMATZ

BE A MAN 169
ROB BUYEA

DRESS APPROPRIATELY 173
MARGO RABB

THERE ARE FIRM RULES IN LIFE 177
THANHHA LAI

DON'T LET THE NEW WORLD CHANGE YOU 181
MITALI PERKINS

ME FIRST 185
LYNDA MULLALY HUNT

ACKNOWLEDGMENTS 191

ABOUT THE CONTRIBUTORS 195

ABOUT THE EDITOR 209

INTRODUCTION
35 WAYS TO BE WHO YOU REALLY ARE

When I went to high school, every 49 minutes a bell would go off, signaling to all of us students that we could now ransack the hallways, notice each other's clothes, look cool in front of gobs of other students, and—eventually—go to our next class. When I became a teacher, the bell (or buzzer, rather, in this school) went off every 43 minutes, and I was surprised to see that life in the hallways was exactly the same—except for a few minor details: guys wore their pants even further below their ulterior cheeks, girls wore their skirts even shorter, and I saw more people making out in the hallways. But the same mixture of coolness, insecurity, desperate hope, and perspiring fear still imbued the hallway scene.

Becoming a teacher made me start wondering if life had to run according to bells like this—bells that tell us when to sit and when to stand, when to speak and when to remain silent, when to laugh and when to cry, and when to simply run away.

Recently I learned that one of my past students had committed suicide. It had been two years since he was in my English class, and yet the vividness of his laughter and his readiness to launch from his seat and volunteer to play the role of Mercutio in *Romeo and Juliet* or to share his original ideas for what makes an ideal school were all still so tangible to me. In truth, my student had an enormous love for life, but finding a way to live life as the person he really was had become impossible for him. He had gotten to the point where it seemed easier to let everything go—all the voices and all the messages and all the tunnels that lead to What You Are Supposed to Be and Want in Life—and instead to stop trying. Because the rules are everywhere, and they're crushing so many people the same way they crushed my student: rules for how a man must act, how a woman must look, who to be friends with, who not to be friends with, how to talk, how to dress, how to think, what to buy, what not to buy, how to feel good, how not to feel good, what grades to get, what college to attend, what to care about, and what love is.

Every day, you're bombarded by what you are supposed to be—and it's always something other than what you are. Be tougher, be thinner, be smarter, be sexier, be funnier, be quieter, be louder, be better dressed, be more aware of what's cool, be better at: everything. When you flip through the pages of a magazine, watch a movie, see a television commercial, play the latest video game, and go to school, the messages are waiting, ready to leap out at you with fangs and claws and devour you.

But here's the thing. The fangs and claws of this Rule Creating Beast aren't sharp and they aren't scary and they don't even look threatening. No. Instead, they look tantalizing and tempting. They look like bean bags and couches you sink into and human-sized pillows that will give you comfort. That's the trick of the Rule Creating Beast. It lunges at you and says, quite clearly, *This is what real life is all about! Do this and you will be happy, cool, and respected.* And because the system of rules is so strong—and because even parents and teachers often obey them—it's hard to find another way to live. It's hard to find out the other option if you stare long enough at the rules facing you and start to see them for the life-sucking, status quo–enabling mechanisms that they really are.

I'll never forget the day when I was a high school sophomore, sitting in Mrs. Van Aulsberg's history class, and she said the name "James Meredith." He was the first black student to be admitted to and then attend the University of Mississippi. The day James Meredith walked onto the college campus, President John F. Kennedy had to call in 500 US Marshals, members of the US Army Military Police, the National Guard, and the US Border Patrol. And all of this military personnel was needed to break one rule—one massively unjust, racist, cruel rule that said that because Mr. Meredith was a black man, he didn't deserve the opportunity to earn a college education at the University of Mississippi. So what did he do? He broke that rule; he said, effectively, *No, I choose to disobey,* and (this time) there was enough support to enable James Meredith to break the rule of an unjust society and live the free life that the founding documents of America guarantee. James Meredith's story has stayed with me since that moment, because the rules are no less severe and no less unjust today. And yet so many of us choose to follow them rather than question them; so many of us accept the way things are rather than gather the army of courage we need to fight it.

Today, the rules we need to break may not always be written in the law books that govern society (though they sometimes still are). But their overpowering nature is no less fierce. The bells (or buzzers) that sound off in our lives and direct our steps need to be broken so that we can do what needs to be done. The words we say, the friends we keep, the clothes we wear, the decisions we make—these need to be choices we make within our authentic selves rather than blindly following what is already happening. James Meredith decided not to listen to the bell that rang and told him he wasn't allowed at a particular college. And there are bells ringing right now in your life—ordering you to act, talk, dress, think, desire, and believe in certain ways—that you need to stop obeying. A lot of those bells are explored in the pages that follow.

You're holding in your hands 200-some-odd pages of distilled wisdom from people who have broken a lot of rules. The authors here share their own experiences of breaking rules or of following rules and wishing they hadn't. Sometimes turning on the television or flipping through a magazine offers a pretty narrow view of ways to live. The authors in this book explode that narrow view. They push the boundaries so far to the sides that a whole lot of other options for living authentically suddenly become possible. Olugbemisola Rhuday-Perkovich describes how listening can be radical; Chris Barton wonders why we're so obsessed with going to college right after high school; Mitali Bose Perkins writes about leaving traditional rules and views behind as you grow and change; Chris Lynch goes toe-to-toe with the notion that a "real man" is tough and rugged and doesn't feel emotion; A. S. King refuses to let herself (or *you*) be shushed to death; Josh Berk laughs at the rule that says you've got to be either a jock or a nerd; Lisa Burstein thunders against the lie that we must all be thin. And many more authors explode other rules that society desperately wants you to believe.

There's a whole world inside of you that is begging to emerge, and this world is going to look magnificently different in every one of you. It's not born by copying the scant options we see in the media or in school or among friends. So here are 35 other ways of living life. Here are 35 rules that you can start breaking right now in order to discover how different from everyone else you can be. And, you might just discover how good it feels to be exactly like you.

Luke Reynolds

BE A JOCK *OR* A NERD.
PICK A SIDE. WE'RE AT WAR.

JOSH BERK

I am the product of not one but two librarians. In other words, I had the most awesome childhood imaginable! I grew up in a house positively bursting with books. From an early age it was made clear to me that books and reading and more generally being smart was a good and important thing to be. So, not surprisingly, I became one of the "smart kids" in school. I got good grades, I liked reading, and I generally nerded it up, nerd-style. There was a poster of Walt Whitman on my wall. When I was in kindergarten! For real.

But the Berks weren't just book lovers. Sports were also big in my house. My dad was (and is) a huge baseball fan. I started with T-ball as soon as I could hold a bat and soon, like generations of American boys before me, became completely obsessed with baseball. And, like generations of American writers before me, I was completely terrible at it. I prayed that I might one day hit a home run or at least possibly reach base on an error or even achieve an illustrious foul tip. But alas, my prayers went unanswered, my bat went back on the rack, and my rump went on the bench.

I was clearly on the path toward being a classic nerd, right? Right. Good at school, bad at sports. But then something happened: I grew. Man, did I grow! Suddenly I had arms like a chimp, I towered over most of my friends, and I could just about dunk a basketball by age 13. This didn't help in baseball, but hey, basketball was OK too. So I went out for the very competitive Freedom High School basketball team and though I still wasn't a star, I made the cut. I made the team. This brought me into a new world. Jock world. My teammates were not the same kids from my honors classes, and they certainly weren't reading poetry for fun like I was.

Fitting in was a challenge. I was constantly hiding something. I wanted very much to fit into that world even though I knew I was living a lie. I didn't listen to the same music they did. There were loud rap songs blasted on the team bus while I quietly listened to Jane's Addiction and Ned's Atomic Dustbin on my portable. (Yes! There really was a band called Ned's Atomic Dustbin. They had two bass players and a song about killing your television. And yes! I used a portable CD player. It was the 1990s. I'm old!) I didn't know what to say on these bus trips, during practice, or even during the games. I didn't know how to act; I didn't even know how to dress to make it in their world. I felt like I had to put everything aside that I enjoyed, at the risk of being embarrassed.

Thoughts rolled through my head constantly: Who am I? Am I a jock or a nerd? Some sort of third thing? Probably everyone wonders these types of things at some point, but for some of us the questions loom especially large. We feel this pressure to fit a predetermined mold, but I simply did not fit. I loved books, *and* sports, *and* that one girl from honors English! *And* that one cheerleader! You can see my mind was very muddled. So I am here to tell you to smash those molds, my friends. The rules of jock world were constraining and limiting.

But, to be fair, it's not just jocks who make the artsy/nerdy kids feel like outcasts. The knife cuts the other way as well. I recently saw a regional high school theater award show where the kid who won best actor announced as part of his speech that before joining drama he used to play lacrosse. There was an audible gasp from the crowd. It was as if a Nobel Peace Prize winner declared during his acceptance address that he enjoyed torturing kittens and farting on babies in his spare time. It simply did not compute with the crowd that this actor type was also a (gasp!) athletic type. I expected pitchforks. *You're not one of us?!* the collective gasp seemed to decry. *Sure* he was. We're all one of us. Don't let anyone tell you otherwise. This took me way too long to learn.

The funny thing is, for how long I struggled with this confusion, the answer was there all along, staring at me from my bedroom wall. The answer comes from Walt Whitman. The word is multitudes. *Embrace your multitudes.* Even if you have to break the rules of clique and caste. Walty (I call him Walty) said it best in his famous poem, *Song of Myself,* which I will now adapt for my needs. That's right! I can dunk and I like poems. Deal with it. (OK, fine, I can't dunk anymore, but still: deal with it.)

Do you contradict yourself?
Go ahead and contradict yourself!
You are large, you contain multitudes . . .
To the secret poet on his way to the game,
Hiding his book of verse under his basketball uniform,
Reading Keats on the bus by the lights of passing cars—
I celebrate you.

To the quiet nerd yearning to rock
All the way out
Blasting polymaths and feedback
I celebrate you too.

It is a new age and we need new hyphenates:
Punk-nerd
Cheerleader-physicist

Emo-jock
Artist-gangsta . . .

No. Forget all that. We don't need hyphenates at all
We don't need labels at all.
The world is not a monochromatic place, it has many tastes.
It is a non-uniform place.
You love cars and physics and drama and videogames
You love the hum of an electric guitar, the swish of a
basketball through a hoop,
Beauty, light and the darkness of words pressed into print.
You love it all,
You live it all.

So stop this day and night with me and remember
That there is not just one way to be
You are large, you contain multitudes.
Go ahead . . .
You're one of us.
We all are.

SHHHHH

A. S. KING

I am only one, but still I am one. I cannot do everything, but still I can do something; and because I cannot do everything, I will not refuse to do something that I can do.
—Helen Keller

You heard it from the minute you were born. You heard it in babyhood when you were sad or hungry or cranky. You heard it in toddlerhood when you were hyper and you hadn't found your volume control yet. You heard it in childhood when you talked more than you ate your dinner or when you played too loudly in the house or when you tried to spout a great idea about how to build a new invention during the nightly news.

They've done studies on how many acts of violence you've seen on TV and how many teaspoons of sugar you eat and how many bases you will clear with your boyfriends and girlfriends before you turn 18, but I don't think anyone has ever done a study on shushing. So I'm going to take a wild guess for the sake of this essay.

By the time you graduate high school, I estimate that the number of times you will be shushed is one million. One million shushes. This includes Shut-ups, Be-quiets, Zip-its, and Hush-nows.

It includes hand signals used in quiet places like church or your sister's cello recital—the zipper-across-the-mouth, the index-finger-straight-up. This includes the bad stuff. The hand-over-the-mouth. The "If you tell anyone about this, I'll kill you." The slap. The backhand. My conclusion: I reckon you've been told to shut up more than anything else so far.

Now don't get me wrong. I'm a mother. I shush my kids all the time. There's nothing wrong with learning boundaries and teaching the appropriate times to speak or make robot noises. However, I think our society goes too far in its quest to make everyone shut up. There's this very dangerous side effect: silence. And while silence is great during your sister's attempt at the sonata in B-flat minor on the cello, on a wider level, silence is a horrible disease that has scarred our society for too long. How would hunger, child abuse, and domestic violence still exist in your neighborhood if it were not for silence? How could genocide and torture and inequality still exist if it were not for silence?

Here's a fact: if you speak up about any of these things, some so-called adults will roll their eyes at you.

"Ha! She wants to cure starvation!"

"Pfffft! He wants to rid the world of genocide!"

"LOL! Good luck with that stopping child abuse and domestic violence crusade!"

We live in cynical, apathetic times. Yes, the ages on their driver's licenses may show they are legal adults, but let me tell you, these people are simply silenced children using cynicism as an excuse to allow their world to stay exactly the same as it was when they arrived. Don't be fooled. At one time in their lives they had dreams and hopes, just like you do. And the only reason they'll laugh at you and me when we try to change the world is because they gave up, gave in, and shut up. Because that's what they were told to do.

I have made it a habit of not doing what I am told to do and I want you to make a habit out of that too. (This does not mean making robot noises at your sister's cello recital.) You have a choice. You can pretend nothing is wrong with your world or you can change the world by saying, "There is something wrong with my world." Don't think other people are going to change it for you. Only you can change your world—your small personal world and your big whole wide world. The first step to that change is: say stuff.

I don't care what you say stuff about. I don't care if it's dogs or cats or kids or the price of cantaloupes in Saskatchewan. If you care, say something. If you're hurting, say something. If you know someone else is hurting, say something. If you can help someone, say something. You have to practice this skill in order to get better at it. The more you point at things and say, "Hey! That's not how things should be!" the more you will notice things that should change. This applies to you, too.

You will get better results if, when you open your mouth, you remember to open your mind as well. In these cynical times, making declarations about who is wrong and who is right and deciding you are the all-knowing expert on the world's problems is only going to make you look silly. Yes, I *know* there are people like that all over TV and radio, but just because they are on TV doesn't make them right. Speak up about truths. About things that are wrong no matter what your politics. It's very hard to go wrong when you are fighting for something, rather than against something. It's very hard to go wrong when you are trying to *help people who are in desperate need of help.*

If you do this, I guarantee you two things: you will feel good, and some people will fight you. They want their comfortable blanket of mind-numbing TV and silence! They do *not* want to think about the starving and suffering people all over the world. They can't do anything to help them, remember? So you're just wasting your time.

Except that you're not. You're doing more than they could, and it makes them feel bad. One out of four of them have suffered some sort of ill treatment themselves and many haven't even been able to speak up about *that* yet, so why would you expect them to help you? They are living proof that there is something wrong with our world. And you and I are living proof that people can speak up and break the silence.

So please. Say it with me: *I will not shut up.* No matter what world you aim to change, you can't do it without your voice. And the rest of us loudmouths need you.

Alone we can do so little; together we can do so much.

—Helen Keller

IT'S BETTER TO BE SAFE THAN SORRY

MATTHEW QUICK

I.

Adults always told us to lock up our bikes whenever we went to the pizza shop or the 7-Eleven. "Even if you're only going inside for a minute—use the bike lock!" they'd say. And when we went to a friend's house, his parents would often ask where we left our bikes. "Don't leave your bikes out front on the sidewalk if you want to keep them!" they'd yell.

I lived in a small suburban South Jersey town called Oaklyn and knew most of my neighbors well. So why the bike theft paranoia?

We were told that the kids from Camden would come and take our bikes.

I don't remember when I first heard about the kids from Camden, but they came up quite a bit when I was in elementary and middle school.

Apparently, the Camden kids invaded our town in pairs. The first partner powered a bike, the second was rumored to ride on the handlebars, and when they saw one of our bikes unlocked, the handlebar rider would leap off, steal, pedal like mad, and escape back into the city of Camden, where none of us would dare to follow.

This was the story, and we lived in constant fear of losing our bikes.

Oaklyn is less than one square mile. I lived there for almost two decades. I never saw strangers casing the streets for unlocked bikes. Not once. Nor did anyone ever steal my ride, even though—because I was a kid—I neglected to lock it up many times. I remember hearing stories about bikes gone missing, but I can't remember any hard facts. "Someone's cousin lost a bike to the kids from Camden," we heard, and we believed it without asking a single question. I don't remember any of my friends losing bikes to the kids from Camden.

Camden is the city that borders Oaklyn. When I was growing up, Camden was considered the most dangerous place in South Jersey. I often heard adults claim that Camden had one of the highest murder rates in the country. Most of the people in Camden did not look like us. They were not of European ancestry. We'd be able to spot them right away if they ever came to our town. We were always looking for them. We were afraid of them. We didn't go into Camden. During the holidays, when our parents took us on the Speedline—through Camden to Center City, Philadelphia—we looked out the train windows and saw that the people of Camden mostly lived in dilapidated row homes. Their city looked dingy, broken, drug-infested, and dangerous. We hoped we wouldn't have to interact with the citizens of Camden, and we didn't.

I am right now—at the time of writing, at the age of 37—sitting in Camden, serving jury duty. Earlier this morning, I got off the Speedline at City Hall and didn't know which way to walk, so I approached the first person I saw. His skin color was different than mine and a tattoo of a dark blue tear leaked from his eye. To be honest, he looked kind of scary and the amateur tattoos on his neck and hands made me wonder if he had spent time in jail.

"Excuse me. Which way is the courthouse?" I asked him.

He flashed a huge smile, and then said, "This way, my man! It's that big building over there. See it?"

I nodded and said, "Thanks."

We exchanged grins.

Middle school me would have been amazed.

High school me would have never asked that man for directions.

II.

When my wife, Alicia, and I landed in Windhoek, Namibia, our friend, a Peace Corps volunteer, greeted us. He had arranged for a taxi to drive us to a hostel. When we saw the troops of baboons next to the highway that leads to the city, we knew we had landed in a new, different world. "Welcome to Africa," our friend said.

My wife and I had just quit our jobs and sold our house to pursue our dream of writing fiction full-time. We had recently traveled in Peru and were beginning a six-week backpacking trip through southern Africa.

"Why Africa?" asked most of the people we knew. These were the same people who had also asked us, "Can you really make a living writing fiction?" Some asked if traveling through southern Africa was dangerous. One acquaintance—who had done business in South Africa—warned us, saying, "It's not safe to take public transportation over there. Be careful!"

When we arrived at the hostel, named the Cardboard Box, we first noticed the tall cement walls.

Inside those walls was a hip open-air space with a pool, bar, fire pit, tent area, and rooms for rent. The guests were mostly friendly Australians, Europeans, and Kiwis—almost all were white people.

Once we were settled in, our Peace Corps friend told us that he would be leaving, which surprised us. He was going to hitch-hike north to fulfill an obligation. The next morning we were to pick up his friend at the airport via taxi, then rent a car, and meet our friend at a northern camping spot before we'd go on safari at Etosha National Park. Before we knew it, he was gone and we were alone in Namibia.

That night I had a panic attack.

I woke up shortly after Alicia and I went to bed. I felt disoriented. I could hear unfamiliar music and people talking in the lounge. Everyone had thick accents. I remembered speaking with the bartender earlier that evening. He was an ex-soldier from England. When I told him we were traveling north and would most likely end up in Zambia, he smiled and said, "You're going to see the *real* Africa then." I wondered what the real Africa would be like. Windhoek already felt strange and unfamiliar. As we had driven through the streets of the city, we didn't see anyone who looked like us. Yet here at the hostel were many people who did. A few dozen white people behind large walls. I remember thinking we had made a mistake coming to Africa. I felt like something bad was going to happen to us. I wanted to go home.

In the morning, I felt better. I reminded myself that I had traveled in South America thrice already and had also been to Europe as many times—that I knew how to be a tourist in a foreign land. My wife was excited to travel north, and so I tried to feed off her enthusiasm and pushed all the bad suspicions deep down back into the subconscious from whence they came.

We managed to pick up our new travel partner at the airport, a man I had never met before, and rent a sedan in Windhoek. When we told the white woman at the car rental place where we were going, she raised her eyebrows at us disapprovingly.

Soon we were traveling north and everything seemed to be going according to plan.

The trouble began when we needed gas.

As we filled our tank at a convenience store, we were approached by a tall, sandy-haired Afrikaner, who looked a lot like we did.

He asked us where we were headed.

When we told him, he pointed to the South African license plates on our rental sedan, and said, "Be careful."

We didn't think too much about it until we met another Afrikaner when we stopped for food.

"How far north are you headed?" he asked us.

"Up to the Angolan border," we said.

He shook his head and said, "You don't want to go there."

"Why?"

He began speaking in a roundabout manner, almost as if he were talking in code. I don't remember exactly what he said, but I do remember his implying that our skin color and the South African license plates would make us a target for Angolan carjackers. Needless to say, we were not happy to get this news.

As we continued to drive north, we ran into several friendly Afrikaners who all warned us to be careful. I got the feeling that they wanted to tell us more, but were holding back, even though they were clearly concerned for our well-being.

When we met our Peace Corps friend that night at the campsite, we told him about the conversations we had with the Afrikaners.

Our friend explained some of the history that fueled their comments. He told us that during apartheid Namibia was divided into north and south by a boundary known as the red line. White people lived in the south. Therefore, even though apartheid was over, many of the Afrikaners had never even traveled north, so how would they know what it was like?

We asked about the carjackings and our friend said that those were almost unheard of these days, and had usually only happened at night. We wouldn't be traveling after sunset.

Needless to say, we were still uneasy.

But the next day we went on safari at Etosha and drove our rental car alongside of elephant herds, zebras, giraffes, kudu, springbok, and so many other beautiful animals. At night we camped in a designated area fenced off to protect us from lions.

The experience was incredible enough to make us forget all about the warnings the Afrikaners gave us.

When we left Etosha and continued north we started to notice that there were fewer and fewer American-style convenience stores. We also noticed more and more huts and cooking fires on the side of the road. "It's like traveling back in time," we all remarked.

Above the red line we stayed with other Peace Corps members who were usually hosted by the most important man in town and therefore lived inside of a compound of sorts. We'd ask for permission to stay, and were allowed to park our sedan inside of a walled or fenced-off area.

When we asked why we were allowed to stay inside the compounds of people we had never met before, we were told it was prestigious for Namibians to host Americans.

It quickly became clear that we were experiencing a culture inaccessible to most Americans, and which would make many Americans extremely uncomfortable. We were completely dependent on the kindness of strangers, sleeping in tents, among people who looked nothing like us, who didn't always speak our language, and who had good reason to mistrust white people.

I've never been more conscious of my skin color and there were times when I felt extremely uncomfortable, especially when people asked questions like, "Where was the USA during apartheid? Why didn't you help us?" We had no answers for them, yet they let us stay in their compounds anyway and often fed us.

When we were in the northernmost part of Ovamboland our friend informed us that we would be attending a wedding celebration near the Angolan border.

"We have no present, nor dress clothes," we said.

"It will be OK."

"We can't drive the car at night!"

"We'll get a ride."

"From whom?"

"Relax."

That night we walked to a bar that seemed to be in the middle of nowhere, ordered beers, and sat at an outdoor table under so many stars. A jukebox was playing and a few people were dancing.

"How will we get to the wedding?" we asked.

"You'll see," our friend replied.

When an old truck pulled up, our friend stood and began speaking with the man inside. After only a minute or so, our friend motioned for us to jump into the bed of the pickup truck.

As we climbed aboard, we asked, "How do you know the driver?"

"I don't," our friend replied. "We're hitchhiking."

And then we were flying across a desertlike terrain, trying to ignore the rust-eaten holes in the floor on which we were sitting.

We approached a compound, the only visible structure for miles and miles. Many cars and trucks were parked outside. People were drinking from large beer bottles. We noticed two things right away: we were the only white people, and many men toted guns.

"It's customary for people to shoot guns at weddings. There are many leftover from the struggle for freedom," our friend said. "But stop staring."

We thanked our driver, who simply smiled and nodded, and then we made our way to the compound entrance. The compound was packed with people and it looked like others were waiting to get in, but we were permitted immediate entrance.

Once inside we were taken to the edge of a gigantic tent and told to wait.

"Are you sure we should be here?" we asked.

"Relax," our friend told us. "Stop thinking like an American. You're in Africa now."

A man brought us a crate of beers and told us to drink up.

We all took one and began to drink.

Before we had two sips, a large man appeared wearing a tuxedo. An *X* of bullets crisscrossed his chest. In his right arm was an AK-47. He thumped my back and said, "Welcome, Americans!" before pointing his assault rifle at the moon and firing for an impossibly long 12 seconds or so.

Ear-splitting noise.

Bullet casings falling.

Fire shooting from the barrel.

Gravity.

What comes up must come down, right? I began to think.

We were in a desert, half a world away from our home, with no cell phone or any way to contact the friends or family who had no idea where we were in Namibia.

Anything could have happened to us.

When the man finished shooting his AK-47 at the stars, he said, "Come. Eat. Drink."

He then led us into a tent, where we discovered it was a double wedding. We were introduced to the brides and grooms and given a ceremonial scoop of homemade liquor that was stored in some type of gourd.

We congratulated the young couples.

We ate.

We drank.

We smiled at the little kids who kept spying on us, laughing at how different we looked.

And I thought about how far away from home I was—how I was surrounded by people who didn't look like me, who didn't think like me—and, yet, I was OK. In fact, I'm not sure I've ever felt more alive in my entire life.

III.

Many people will tell you that it's not safe to travel the way we did in Namibia—that we were foolish and took unnecessary risks. And to be truthful, Alicia and I are not always so brave. We're actually pretty conservative when it comes to risk taking. Our time in southern Africa definitely tested our limits. And yet, it also changed the way we view the world in many ways.

Mark Twain once wrote, "Travel is fatal to prejudice, bigotry and narrow-mindedness, and many of our people need it sorely on these accounts. Broad, wholesome, charitable views of men and things cannot be acquired by vegetating in one little corner of the earth all one's lifetime."

I completely agree.

Travel—leaving your literal and metaphorical neighborhood— often means abandoning your comfort zone, taking risks, and trusting strangers. When you travel the way we did in Namibia, you must trust that most people are basically good.

Bikes are stolen every day. Travelers are sometimes robbed. Crime exists everywhere, albeit in varying degrees. Racism is unfortunately alive and well. Carjackings do occur in America and Africa. And people are shot daily, all over the globe. The world can be a dangerous place—no doubt. And this is why we often form small groups and alliances in an attempt to protect our loved ones and ourselves from danger. I suppose it's instinctual. We say, *It's better to be safe than sorry. Don't take risks. Herd up. Stay in your town, with the people you know, the people who are very much like you. Don't talk to strangers. Don't trust people who are different. Don't risk injury. Don't live enough to become who you were meant to be, because it's better to be a seed stored safely away for the future than to be alive and in bloom. It's better to be safe than sorry.*

I used to think like this when I was a kid growing up in Oaklyn, New Jersey.

But I have since learned that life is often messy, and that if you want to live an interesting and fulfilling existence, taking calculated risks—not rash, ridiculous chances, because there is a difference—is requirement number one. Being in bloom means opening yourself up to the world. It means risking petals.

When I was a kid I never dreamed I'd travel to Peru and Ecuador, take a riverboat up the Amazon to the jungle town of Pevas, hike Machu Picchu twice, swim with the sea creatures that hang out on and around the Galapagos Islands, hike the Grand Canyon, go white water rafting on the Zambezi, and make my living writing fiction. I never dreamed I'd do these things because the adults in my life had never had—nor would they want to have—such experiences. I used to be afraid of the world, of taking risks, because I was taught to be fearful. But somewhere along the way I discovered it's *not* always better to be safe than sorry—that sometimes the best life experiences happen when you're aware of your heartbeat and your palms are a little sweaty.

LISTENING IS A WASTE OF TIME

OLUGBEMISOLA RHUDAY-PERKOVICH

There used to be a show on MTV with the tagline "You think you know ... but you have no idea."

When I was 16, I *knew* that I was a future magazine editor living, sleekly single, on Manhattan's Upper West Side surrounded by stainless steel appliances and marble countertops, many worshipful boyfriends, and wool tights that never itched.

I had no idea.

I was all about "doing something" as a teen. I wanted to Make Things Happen. Make. My. Mark. In that fantasy, I did a lot of purposeful walking through the city streets while everyone slow-clapped just because my arrival meant that the party would indeed get started. I was an achiever, proud of good grades that got my (long) name on lists and certificates. I read a lot of Jane Austen and dreamed of being an Accomplished Woman. Everybody would see The Things I'd Done.

My attitude toward activism was the same. I mean, the word was, basically, *active*, right? You *did* things. My mother encouraged us to be aware of systems of injustice, of areas of need in our community and beyond. We marched. We wrote letters. I learned to speak up! Take a stand! And pick a side.

Today, there are more and more voices demanding our allegiance. It's like you just finished the days of pounding clay and *Sesame Street,* and all of a sudden you are being asked to Do Something. To do Many Things, Now. Everything is urgent. A multitude of campaigns for your attention fall out on you when you open the day's closet door. Adults, friends, technology, and media . . . everyone seems to be telling you to do something, to say something, to be yourself! Stand up! Sit in! Speak out!

Do you ever just stand up and speak out just for the sake of doing something? Just because people tell you to? I did. I do. I get a call, an e-mail, a letter that I skim just to find out what they want me to do so I can do it and get on to doing the next thing. I am directed to blog posts that have angered some and outraged many, and I scan quickly, looking for something that I can reference in the comments. I compose a response before I've even finished reading. I answer before I've even really listened to the whole question.

At a conference about the teaching of writing, one of the speakers shared this quote from writer and educator Donald Murray: "I must somehow find time to listen so I hear what I have to say." When there is so much shouting, so much that "needs" to be done, and done now, I've learned to stop. And listen. I've learned that "radical listening" is often uncomfortable, like wool tights on dry skin, and sometimes as shockingly painful as a bad breakup—but when we listen, truly listen to the voices within and without, it is an act of real courage. It is listening toward transformation. It lets us see the preciousness that comes from listening to the spaces between the lines. And it can change the world.

When we get so wrapped up in making sure our voices are heard, we become the only voices we hear. "You're not *listening* to me!" I say in arguments with my husband, impatiently waiting for him to stop talking so that I can get on with saying the next thing I want to say. But when I listen, not just for my own echo but for that still, small voice at my center, I am surprised. Not only do I find myself and what I really mean, but I'm introduced to selves I hadn't met before and able to say the words I'd never even dreamed of saying (I'm sorry, perhaps?). I look at the lives of people I admire for many reasons: Dr. Martin Luther King Jr., Mahatma Gandhi, Mother Teresa, Malcolm X, Nelson Mandela. My mom Patricia, my sister Kikelomo. They all had periods of intense, often forced listening. They all took time in the uncomfortable silence and came out on the other side, strong. Came out giving the rest of us strength.

We want to answer the calls to action, quiet the cries for help. Sometimes it seems as though the wrongs will never be right. People are hungry, at war, grieving, and unloving. You might feel like there's more to do than can ever possibly be done. That what you're even thinking about is so infinitesimally small, so insignificant, that it's not even worth considering, let alone actually doing.

Science fiction writer Theodore Sturgeon wrote, "Sometimes the world's too much to live with and a body sort of has to turn away from it to rest."

Radical listening turns you away, and then back again. It keeps your ears open to that voice of hope that tells you that baby steps are still steps forward. Radical listening takes time to discover and consider. Radical listening takes you on voyages of discomfort, into the unknown, to find the answers you'd never thought of, the solutions you didn't know were there. When you listen to the beginning, middle, and end of the story, you are transformed. And that transformation can change the world. Only you may know about the choice that put you on a particular path, only that person who sat across from you knows how much your smile and kind words got them through another day, but when you listen for what your world really needs, you can have impact. Never doubt that. You can't help but make your mark.

With radical listening, I allow myself the room to ask the questions that don't always have answers, to wonder if making this $10 donation will only make a difference in how good I feel about myself, or if spending 20 minutes wondering if I should add another exclamation point to the "I agree!" I post to a message board is really a valuable use of my time. Radical listening asks: What do I really think about this? What do I know? What do I want to know? Radical listening can make those who want you to do something uncomfortable, even angry because you're "not doing anything." But you are. Radical listening can deconstruct and reconstruct and rock your world.

Stop. Look. Listen.

Sit. Lie down. Just be. Don't try to think of something. Or anything. Or this thing. Or that thing. Listen hard, and let the thoughts that have been tiptoeing around the perimeters of your soul, waiting patiently to be welcomed in, let them whisper in your ear and help you decide if you really want to be just friends, if college is in your future, if your mother was right, or if you need to think about it some more. Listen without always having to speak in response. Listen first, so you know that it's better to be loving than to be liked.

I like to knit and do needlework; it quiets my mind and awakens my spirit until I "remember" things I didn't know I knew. Remember that clay? How you could spend ages just squishing and rolling and holding it? Or building towers of blocks, elaborate and rickety, that took ages to construct even though you knew that they would be cleaned up or knocked down in an instant. But that process was precious. It's even official! Research has shown that through play, children "take pieces of experiences and transform them into something new, reordering things in terms that make sense to them, and gaining mastery over the challenges they've encountered." Everyone may be telling you: *Grow up. Be responsible. Stop fooling around.* But radical listening, in all its maturity, needs time to play around with things in your head.

I live in New York City, where there is a lot of noise. I hear my neighbors laughing, the baby upstairs wailing, passersby bickering, trains rumbling . . . the city itself sputtering and shouting time forward. A lot is making its presence known. There is literally a breathtaking array of racial, ethnic, and cultural groups squeezed into the same space. I love it. I hear it. I listen to it.

Don't get me wrong—I don't skip through the streets with my rainbow coalition of friends, our elbows linked and our smiles bright. But paying attention, listening to how we are all living in this city forces me to walk for a while with the right shoe on the left foot. I listen, and I learn to appreciate the unfamiliar for what it is. I learn to listen to the voices that say things differently, at different volumes, but who speak a compelling language of the soul. Maybe I understand right away, I totally relate; maybe it's like parachuting into a new country, arms flailing and legs kicking, disoriented and gasping, with even the words that I do know escaping me in a surge of self-consciousness and fear. But I can choose to keep listening, and come to know that even if I don't hear myself in the other voice, you and I will find each other; we'll create something new together and who we are will remain beautifully and wholly intact. We can listen to each other without either one of us disappearing.

So I stop. I look. I listen.

Then I write.

As James Thurber said, "Don't get it right; get it written."

I wouldn't be doing my job as I see it if I didn't encourage you to write about what you listen to. Writing can lead you to radical listening. It can take the ideas and epiphanies and sorrows and delights that have settled on your soul, and give them new life. True life. Write however you like and however you can—on scraps of paper, in a beautiful keepsake notebook, using digital technology, through art—play with your thoughts, listen to and collaborate with them to tell your story.

I write to create opportunities to listen. To step outside of myself and my affinities into completely unknown people and worlds. If I listen well enough, I can get to a place where it's more important for me to know another heart than to find justification for my own feelings, or to prove my point.

I write to make meaning and listen between the lines. To move, as author bell hooks says, "from silence into speech."

I write to learn things I didn't know I needed to know. I write to really listen to your story, and mine. I write because I have faith, and because I have doubts. I listen because I adore the magic and mystery of life, and then I write to imagine and remember. I write because listening is itchy and often excruciating but writing keeps me listening for the joy beyond the happiness, the justice beyond what's fair.

If you haven't guessed yet, I don't exactly have that life that my 16-year-old self dreamed of. Not even close. And I am so glad. (Except for the tights thing.) So be authentic! Be full-bodied! Tell your story and make your voice heard. Listen to know what you really have to say; the when, why, and how of what to do. Take a stand that you believe in. Just listen at the beginning, the middle, and go on to the end, and don't leave off. Radical listening can help you, as it's helped me, take small but strong steps toward not just doing something but doing it with more wisdom, more purpose, and more love, even if it takes a few do-overs along the way.

NEVER BE ALONE

FRANCISCO X. STORK

This was an unspoken rule of my youth. I never heard it said out loud, but it was always there. Another variation of this rule was the belief that you needed to fill your leisure time with activities that involved others. To be alone, especially on a Friday or Saturday night, was to be a loser.

I don't think I broke this rule on purpose, at least not in the beginning. Being alone is something that just naturally happened. It wasn't until my teenage years that I found out it was something to be avoided. I am an only child, and not having brothers or sisters forced me to create my own entertainment. For as long as I can remember there were imaginary dialogues with invented characters. Games that others played with partners I played with make-believe persons. There was also the early-discovered joy of reading. My grandfather's encyclopedia, which I inherited when I was growing up in Mexico, became my constant friend from the first grade on. Then there were the comic books that I started collecting at age seven. Every Sunday I was allowed to buy one comic book. My favorite ones were called *Vidas Ilustres* and they were the biography of a saint or some other illustrious historical figure. Alone in my room I dreamt of a life of sacrifice and heroism.

It was not until I was a teenager and we had moved to the United States that I became more and more aware of the stigma of being alone. To be alone was a deficiency, it indicated that something was lacking, it pointed toward something that need-ed to be remedied. For the first time I began to feel lonely. Even worse, being alone was the same as being rejected. I was alone not because I wanted to be alone but because no one wanted to be with me. Being alone, being separate, being different, were all the same. And there was an element of truth in this indiscriminate lumping. I felt separate, distant from my school peers. I was not comfortable in the group and the group was not comfortable with me. Suddenly it hurt to be alone.

I remember one day when being alone was indeed full of pain. There was Betty. Incredibly beautiful Betty, I had a crush on her. One day I managed to ask her to a dance and to my great surprise she agreed. All week long, I planned, dreamed of Saturday. Then on Saturday morning there was a telephone call. It was Betty.

"I'm sorry," she said, "I can't go out with you tonight."

"Why?"

"My parents won't let me go out with Mexicans."

That night I started writing. I had written before, of course—school compositions, writings meant for others. But that Saturday night, while others were at the dance, I *chose* to be alone and write for myself. That night I wrote about the unfairness of it all. How hard it was to be rejected and for what reason? Her parents didn't even know me. Feelings were poured into that green notebook.

It is hard to pinpoint the exact moment when I decided to dedi-cate my life to writing. The conviction that writing was my purpose in life grew slowly. But that Saturday night marked a beginning of sorts. It was the moment when solitude became a choice, an impor-tant part of the person I was and the person I wanted to become.

This initial choice to be alone evolved throughout the years. Yes, at the beginning there was a certain defiance to my aloneness, a kind of "I'll show them" stance. I choose to be alone because I am different. I was lonely in my solitude, but that was the price I paid for being special. I was alone with my pride and resentment. I was not happy, but I was not meant to be happy. Happiness was for those who were afraid to break the "unspoken rule."

When I was 45 years old, I started to write fiction. I had been keeping a journal since that day in high school when I first chose to be alone, but now the journal became about someone else, a character I invented. Writing my first novel marked the second phase of my stance with solitude. Now for the first time, I was not separating myself from others by being alone, I was reaching out. It wasn't just expression that I sought through my writing but also communication—a communication that could only take place in solitude.

Through the years I have found a way to be alone and not be separate. Solitude is necessary for writing. But more than that, it is the source of all true sharing. You need to have something to give in order to give. And your gifts can only be gathered and collected in solitude. I have found a way to turn my alone time into a source of giving. The rule of "thou shalt not be alone" is a rule that I consciously break for the sake of others.

It took me many years to find the right way to be alone. I see it now as part of who I am and part of my purpose in life. It took a long time to understand that living is this constant motion of taking in and giving out, that both the closing and the opening are part of the same process. When I was young, I tended to see things as either/or (*either* alone *or* with others). Now I see the both/and of life (*both* alone *and* with others).

How you are when you're alone is all that matters. What's your stance in solitude? Are you rejecting or are you accepting? Can you do both? Can you be alone and still love? If you are alone with bitterness, nothing beautiful will grow in you. Be alone with love. Break the rule for a reason. Break the rule for love.

DON'T TELL

NEESHA MEMINGER

I was born in a village in rural Punjab. We had no electricity or running water and getting a snake in the house was about as common as most people finding a mouse in their apartment in New York City, where I currently live. Punjab has one of the highest rates of both female foeticide and bride burning in all the states of India. The reasons for this are many and complicated (for a comprehensive look at how British land rights laws substantially increased culturally sanctioned violence against women, Veena Talwar Oldenburg's book, *Dowry Murder: The Imperial Origins of a Cultural Crime* is an excellent read), but the attitudes and biases that have their roots in misogyny, coupled with greed, have affected every single Punjabi girl and woman I've met.

As the only daughter in a family dominated by males, I received no encouragement to speak my mind or express myself. The cardinal rule in our home was: Respect your elders. The natural extensions of that rule were Respect authority, Don't ask questions, Don't speak up, and Never question your elders.

I have broken every single one of those rules. Sometimes, the consequences were harsh, with punishments that have left lasting, lifelong impacts. Other times, I was able to break the rule with the belief that the outcome was worth the inevitable wrath of my parents and other authority figures.

I spoke out in a lot of small ways at home when I was a little girl. I questioned why lighter skin was more beautiful—not only in my mother's eyes but to many Indian people. This was a natural question since I was not, relatively speaking, a light-skinned child. My brother, who was often compared to me, was far lighter skinned and therefore more beautiful. I learned early that not being beautiful was a grave disaster for a girl child—as was any physical "blemish" not considered beautiful. So I strived to be smart—to make up for what I lacked by excelling academically. I managed to do well at school, but I would never be allowed to forget the stain that blotted my marketability as a future bride.

That was the first thing I questioned: Why am I ugly to you?

The next thing was: Why are my brothers more valued than I am?

The answers I received were never adequate. They left me with more questions and had lots of gaping holes in their logic. So I began my journey of searching for answers. In high school, I tried my best to abide by the ideals of the dominant structure. I tried to be pretty according to its dictates. The problem was that what western culture deemed beautiful was, at times, in stark opposition to what was considered beautiful in my own home (not including the light-skinned thing). My parents wanted me to "look Indian." My father wanted me to eat more while the magazines around me told me I should be thinner than was healthy for any teen girl. I wanted to look like my friends. And as I bucked their rules and did what I wanted to anyway, whether it was in front of them or behind their backs, I still struggled with the conflicting ideals within my own psyche.

More questions: What, really, was "attractive"? What did I think was attractive? Did I even know? And why did I care?

Well, I cared because at school, being accepted was social survival. And at home, it meant having or not having the love and approval of my mother. It also meant the approval, or not, of the Indian community, upon which my parents placed heavy importance.

In dealing with the school system in Canada, I was introduced to race dynamics. I discovered quickly that being Indian meant being dirty, smelly, less-than, undesirable, uncool, reviled. It meant hostility from my peers and some teachers, acts of violence toward people who looked like me, it meant living as an unwelcome guest in a land that was now "home."

Again—questions: Why do you revile me? Why do you want me to go "back" to where I came from? Why do you think I am less human than you?

I learned that in my new home, people had preconceived notions of who I was as soon as I walked into a room—based on my name and skin color. I found that many of the things I learned at home around being a girl applied to being brown in the larger, Canadian landscape—I was expected to be less-than, docile, rule-following, complicit in my own oppression. A "good girl." A "good minority." I was not to create any waves and I was to be grateful for whatever rights were not taken away, or stomped on entirely.

It was like neurosurgery to look at and take apart all the carefully placed wires meant to control me as a little brown girl. They were put there through centuries of perfecting—generations of trial and error—and they were meant to make me a complicit, pliable, receptive young woman who would continue the cycles of male preference and male domination, white supremacy and racism.

Except...I questioned. And I kept questioning, even after beatings and punishments and various sorts of deprivation. Still, I questioned. And I searched. I dug. I kept digging and I moved farther and farther away from those wires meant to keep me quiet and in place. And soon, I was somewhere out of reach, where I could question in peace. I could follow my trail of questions to answers that made more sense. And, most important, I could follow my trail of questions to others who'd endured similar wrath for questioning. And they were still questioning. I found like-minded souls.

And in this community of like-minded souls, I could spread my wings, learn from their journeys, share mine, and we could grow together.

The first book I ever wrote was called *Tell*. It was an epic tale of three generations of Indian women and the impact that misogyny, migration, male domination, racism, and oppressive socio-economic conditions had on their relationships; how they had bonded or divided according to forces that had nothing to do with the women themselves.

The book never sold. Most publishers wouldn't touch it. One said they worried it might be too "inciteful." I put that one in the drawer, but it was important for me to have written it. It was also fitting that my first attempt at creative expression was called *Tell* after a lifetime of being told to keep quiet.

What I do now as I write novels is what I've always done: tell the truth as I see it. It's not always welcomed or met with approval, just as it wasn't when I was a child, but now I am not afraid of the punishment. (Yes, even as adults, there are forms of punishment to navigate. There are many ways people are kept in line, whether through blacklisting a "difficult" author so that she faces more challenges to publishing and promoting her books, or through undermining her credibility if she challenges the status quo. Sometimes the repercussions are severe, and sometimes they are more quiet.) Speaking up has always been about soul survival for me. When I allow untruths to guide my steps, I begin to slowly die inside. I become sad, depressed, joyless. And when this happens, I know I need to change direction somewhere in my life.

That's when I have to go inside myself, sit quietly, and listen to the pain. Emotions are units of information: if you are angry, you have been violated in some way—cast around in your memory for when that might have been; if you are sad, there has been a loss—again, trawl your mind for what you have lost and grieve it. Feeling the pain helps it to go away. It's not easy and it's not fun, but it's healthy. And I guarantee you it gets easier the more you do it. The pain decreases in intensity and then you are bigger than it. You can manage it. You can decide when you deal with it and when you put it away for later. But don't ignore it. Whatever you ignore keeps coming back until you face it head on. Once you move *through* it, instead of *away* from it, you become stronger, more whole—and way more powerful.

My feelings tell me what I need to do next. How I need to change the direction I'm going in. The people, places, things I need to cut out of my life. Where I need to spend more time, more energy. The hardest part is becoming quiet enough to listen.

When I was growing up, the whole world seemed to tell me I was valueless, worthless. I was a dark-skinned girl child in a world that valued light-skinned or white men and boys. The stories all around me told me that. Everything I saw on television, in magazines, on book covers and within books, in movies and on billboards—all told me I was of lesser value. At home, that message was reinforced from the light-skinned images of the ten male gurus my mother prayed to, to the Fair and Lovely ads on Indian television shows and in Indian magazines.

But I didn't buy it. I questioned. I spoke up. I listened to my truth all the way through it, no matter how hard the messages around me tried to stomp it out. I stood fast in the whipping winds that come with opening something painful, facing what is hard or impossible to endure. Somewhere inside, I kept hearing that whisper that said, *That's not true.* It was a feeble whisper, for sure, but it was there. It's inside all of us. We all know we are valuable and of tremendous worth. We are here to contribute all we have to offer, and within each of us is an infinite amount of learned wisdom—at any age.

So, dare. Dare to question. Dare to challenge the messages around you that you don't agree with. Even if that means disagreeing with those you love.

There will always be those around you who will want you to shut up or be quiet. But here's my advice to you: *Don't.* Don't run away from what is hard and don't shy away from saying what you know others might not want to hear. You are loved and valued beyond your wildest imagination—exactly as you are. Listen to that inner voice, and listen to your feelings. All the guidance you'll ever need is there.

DON'T QUIT

CARL DEUKER

Quitters never win and winners never quit. You hear it all the time, and it sounds like it should be true. And sometimes it is true ... but not always. Nothing in life is simple.

You've heard the story a million times on television. Some college or pro athlete will be interviewed on ESPN and within five minutes he'll be telling you about his old high school coach. "At the time I thought he was a real jerk. He was always on me. I hated him. But now I look back and realize he was the best thing that ever happened to me."

So how do you know if your screamer/coach is actually a good person helping you build your character, a person you'll thank all your life, or a bad person tearing you down, who you'll curse till your dying day? How do you know whether to quit or to hang in there?

It's not always an easy call, but there are a couple of basic questions that can guide you: *What does the coach want from you? Is he looking for wins, or is he looking for effort?*

Here's why it matters.

You can't guard LeBron James.

You can't.

And you might not be able to guard the small forward on the rec team from the community center two miles away. That guy may be too big or too fast or too quick for you. Or he might be all three. But you *can* try to guard him. You can try from tip-off to the final whistle. If you're overmatched but you give it your all, and your coach still screams at you, then he's looking for wins and you should be looking for the door.

But here's where it gets tricky. Because before you walk out that door, you need to do some serious soul-searching. If your effort has been lagging, if you've been feeling sorry for yourself because you're not a starter or a star, if you've been loafing at practice, if you've been blaming the refs, if you've been dogging it in any way—then your coach is right to be on your case. He's challenging you to take your eyes off the scoreboard and turn them in on yourself. He's telling you that effort matters more than score.

There's no failure where there's effort—ever. You can lose 60–30, and if you hung in there and fought to the final whistle, then you succeeded. You can win 60–30, but if you didn't play the game the way it was meant to be played, then you stopped respecting yourself, and you stopped respecting the game, and you failed.

Your goal is to become the best player that you can be. Maybe that means you'll end up a professional athlete who makes the great play to win the championship. Maybe that means you'll be a second stringer who never sees a minute of playing time but helps her team by pushing the starters hard at practice.

The point isn't whether your name ends up in the headlines or at the very bottom of the box score, whether you put up big numbers or no numbers at all. Where you end up isn't as important as how you got there. Were you a good teammate? Were you a good opponent? Did you play the game right?

If that coach who's driving you hard is looking at your effort, then stay the course. He's building you up, preparing you for life and all it's going to throw at you. But if all he sees is the final score, and if he's ripping you apart no matter how much effort you give him, then don't let him tear you down.

Quit.

BE CLEAN!

GARY D. SCHMIDT

Let me start with this: I don't think bowling is that great a sport. The object of the game, of course, is to throw a large ball down a long alley and hit 10 pins—and to do the same thing in the same way 12 times in a row. I get the difficulty of this. I really do. But the business of trying to do this time and time again is, well, unattractive to me. Always has been.

But when our youth pastor announced that our high school group had been invited to an All-Night Bowlathon, I bit. I mean, being out all night with friends, staying up past dawn, the promise of lots of coffee and bad food—it all sounded pretty good. Even with the bowling.

"And just to let you know," said the youth pastor, "the bowling lanes probably won't have enough shoes for everyone. You'll probably be bowling in your socks."

This puzzled me. There were only 20 or so of us. Why would there not be enough shoes?

And on little moments like that, we sometimes look back and think, Why didn't I see that coming? But we never see it coming. And I had no idea how much was going to end very soon.

*   *   *   *   *

On the designated night, we gathered at church after supper, joking about how none of us had gotten enough sleep last night, how we hadn't eaten much supper so we could eat the horrible hot dogs, how we'd be buzzed on coffee by the 14th game, how we could take bets on how many gutter balls Alicia would throw, how Trevor—the only bowler among us—could probably go for a perfect game if he had enough shots at it. We squeezed into the van—all 20 of us, and it wasn't that big a van—and we headed out as darkness began to fall, and the streetlights came on, and normal folks were sitting down to Walter Cronkite.

Trevor began to calculate how many games we could get in. If we got to the Bowlathon at 7:30, and bowled until 7:30 the next morning, and bowled four games an hour, and took occasional breaks for the bad food and coffee and biology, then maybe we could get in, say, 40 games.

"Maybe," I said.

"Maybe 45," he said.

"Just don't go to the bathroom," I said.

"I think I could do that," Trevor said. He really wanted a perfect game.

But at 7:30 we were still driving, and at 8:00 we were still driving, because it turned out that the Bowlathon was way out on Long Island. I watched Trevor make his new depressing calculations every 15 minutes.

It was almost 8:30 when the van stopped in the parking lot of a large high school—a parking lot filled with many other vans, vans marked on the side with the names of churches from all over Long Island. Crowds of kids like us walked toward the school, looking—like us—sort of bewildered.

We asked our youth pastor who all these kids were.

"Well ..." he said.

We asked if there were bowling lanes in the high school.

"Well ..." he said.

This was not encouraging.

Trevor looked at his watch. "Maybe 35 games. Don't drink any coffee."

We walked, sort of silently, through the glass doors, and through a long lobby, and past folks with bright yellow T-shirts who were clapping enthusiastically as we walked by, and finally into a massive auditorium, where happy Bible songs were playing: "Rise and shine and give God the glory glory." The yellow T-shirts sang along encouragingly.

Our youth group sat together down by the front since the auditorium had filled in quite a bit, and Trevor sat beside me and looked at his watch. 8:40.

More kids came in.

More happy Bible songs. "If you're happy and you know it clap your hands …"

8:50.

Trevor making new calculations.

And finally, 9:00, and a bright yellow T-shirt on a guy way too old to wear a bright yellow T-shirt leaped—kind of—onto the stage and held up a mic.

"Good evening," he said.

"I said, 'Good evening!'" he tried again.

We said good evening.

"I suppose you're all eager to be bowling, right?"

"Yes," we all answered. Especially Trevor.

"And you're wondering what you're doing here, right?"

We were indeed.

"I'll tell you that in a bit. But first, let's sing praise to our awesome God."

And canned happy Bible music piped through the speakers as the bright yellow T-shirts came onto the stage together, grinning like all get out, clapping like they were the Big Show and weren't we glad to be here.

"Let's all stand," said the guy on the stage.

We did.

We were still standing a half hour later after a battery of happy Bible songs that would have taken down Jericho two, three times over.

I think Trevor was almost crying.

When we sat down, I leaned over and said, "Maybe 30?"

He shook his head.

"Wasn't that great?" said the guy on the stage.

"I said, 'Wasn't that great?'" he tried again.

We said it was great.

"I promised you I'd tell you why you're here," said the man. "That's what I'm going to do right now. You're here to save your souls," he said. "Oh you'll get your bowling, don't you worry about that. But don't you think the state of your soul is a whole lot more important than your bowling score?"

I—who couldn't care less about my bowling score—think I hated him, this bright yellow man with his snake oil voice and his happy happy happy music, and his deception, and now him wanting us to be glad that we'd been deceived. "God wants you to have a good time," he said, "but he wants you to have a clean heart first."

He leaned down to the first row, and someone—on cue—handed him a Bible. A very big Bible. But he didn't need to open it. He knew what he wanted to say, and he didn't need a crib.

"Let's talk first about your rock and roll," he said.

I leaned down toward our youth pastor. Someone had given him a bright yellow T-shirt and he was wearing it over his own polo. He wasn't looking at anyone but the guy on the stage.

"Do you know what rock and roll does to you?" the guy on the stage asked.

I actually didn't, but he did. It made me unclean, he said. I wasn't sure how Simon and Garfunkel did this, but I guess the guy on the stage knew.

A while later: "Do you know what comics do to you?" the guy on the stage asked.

I actually didn't, because I only read *Classics Illustrated*, but the guy on the stage knew. It made me unclean.

A while later: "Do you know what books do to you? Books like *The Exorcist* and *The Grapes of Wrath* and a whole lot of others?"

I thought I knew this one, since I'd read *The Exorcist* and fallen asleep at that last chapter where everything goes haywire. But it turns out I didn't know. But the guy on the stage did. Books made me unclean.

"Do you know what smoking does to you?"

Well, he might have been right on this one, I suppose.

This went on for a long time. It involved passionate tears on his part at opportune times, which showed his concern for our clean hearts, I guess. It involved long quotations. It even involved swelling organ chords that came from I don't know where when the really passionate parts were invoked.

Trevor, all this while, was calculating. Every so often I looked at him, and he shook his head. We were below 20 by now.

But things looked better when the guy on the stage announced that he only had one thing more to talk about, the most important thing, the thing we all had to pay attention to, the thing that more than anything dirtied up the heart of a teenager.

He wanted to talk about sex.

This got our attention, probably because most of us had never heard this word used in a churchy situation before. But the guy on the stage nodded. Yes sirree, he was going to talk about sex. He really was. And did we know what the Bible said about sex? The Bible said in Genesis that sex was original sin. That's what Genesis said. Original sin. That means that all those other sins he'd been talking about started with this. Sex. Original sin. He paused to let us think about this.

So I did think about it, and I figured that somehow, he must have gotten hold of a different translation of Genesis, since I'd read it, and I didn't remember anything about sex being original sin. I almost raised my hand, but I didn't think the guy on the stage was taking questions.

For a preacher, he had a lot to say about sex and original sin and about a clean heart and about American teenagers and us in particular. And I guess it must have been sort of riveting—all about how it started with talking quietly together, then holding hands, then going on walks, and then, boy oh boy, then, all hell was likely to break loose, and we'd be unclean like nobody's business. You can see how a description of the transactions of damnation would get your attention. But the climax was yet to come, and it came around midnight—"Maybe 15," said Trevor. The guy on the stage said that he wanted us all to do something for him. Then he thought a minute, and he said, No, it wasn't for him. It was for Jesus. Here's what he wanted us to do for Jesus.

"When I tell you to, all you guys in the auditorium, I want you to stand up. That's right. I want you to stand up. And I want you to hold your right hand out into the air and swear as if your hand was on this Bible"—he held it up high—"that you will never, ever touch a girl until you have married her. That's right. Never touch a girl ever. Because we know where that leads—you hold a girl's hand, and you dirty up your heart, and it doesn't take a whole lot of imagination to know where you go from there. So I want you to stand up. Make this your number one rule in life: 'I will never touch a girl until I have married her.' Are you ready?"

I wasn't ready.

I was angry.

Three hours on a lie. Three hours and he didn't even get the Genesis stuff right. Three hours to promise that I wouldn't touch a girl? Never hold her hand? Never touch her shoulder? Never hug her? Never kiss her? Really?

And it wasn't as if I was this guy running around high school practicing up for original sin. I was sort of nerdy. I read books. I played tennis and chess. I liked to run. I was sort of focused on college coming up. I didn't look for shadowy crevices in the school architecture to smoke and make out. I felt sort of brave when I just talked to a girl, kind of quietly.

And at the moment, there wasn't a girl who was going to let me hold her hand anyway.

But dang it, three hours on a lie.

And Genesis never says that holding hands makes an unclean heart.

"Are you ready?" said the guy on the stage. "Really ready to do this for Jesus?"

I knew this wasn't for Jesus.

And now I was ready.

"Stand up for Jesus and swear!"

I think every guy in the auditorium stood up. The youth pastor, the guys in my youth group, the guys in every other youth group, the guys in the bright yellow T-shirts who probably were clean already but were standing to show solidarity. Even Trevor. They all stood up.

They all stood up to swear never to touch a girl.

The number one rule in life.

Every single guy.

Except me.

It must have been pretty obvious to those around me.

"Is every guy standing?" asked the guy on the stage.

It was a blessing that no one ratted me out. I'm not sure what would have happened.

But even so, I felt scorn and disdain and horror and disgust around me. I felt stares from behind, and beside, and from those who turned around in the row ahead. They looked at me like I was original sin with no bright yellow T-shirt, and they leaned away from the leper who could just as well have been shouting "Unclean! Unclean!" as he was reaching forward to grope toward them.

They raised their right hands. They spoke their number one rule in life. They said it again, in unison. And again. The voices of the clean filled the auditorium.

Except mine.

"Now we'll pray," said the guy on the stage. "I want every eye closed, every body still."

And when every eye was closed and every body still, I got up and walked out. Those around me were careful that I didn't touch them. Unclean, after all.

I waited for the youth group by the van. No one said anything to me when we got in.

Not even the youth pastor.

We got to the bowling lanes a little after 1:00 AM. I drank bad coffee, ate two hot dogs with onions and chili, and then bowled in my socks with some girls I didn't know from another church. Nine games. Then a couple of guys with cigarettes at the corners of their mouths closed the place down and chased us out. "You left a hell of a mess!" they called after us. "Who do you think is going to clean this up?"

It was the last time I went to any of the youth group gatherings.

We avoided each other in church services.

Even Trevor and I fell away. I guess he had a lot to worry about, all that cleanliness, and who knows who I had touched on my way into the sanctuary.

The youth pastor made a couple of halfhearted attempts, but I guess he figured I was lost and so he gave up. Or maybe he just knew that there had been some original sin that night—but it wasn't sex.

I went away to college in the fall, and never saw any of them again.

*   *   *   *   *

Not many years later—in fact, only a handful of years later—I met Anne. We were both standing on the top floor of the John Hancock Tower in Boston, looking at the clean lines of the distant White Mountains of New Hampshire.

We talked quietly and privately.
We went for a long walk through the lovely streets of Boston.
We held hands the whole time.
We still do.

NEVER TALK ABOUT RELIGION

SARA ZARR

Have you ever been told that you should never talk about politics and religion in polite company? I have. And though I'm not entirely sure what "polite company" is, it doesn't seem like very many people follow this rule anymore, at least as far as politics. You can hardly get through a day without hearing someone talk about politics.

Religion, now that's a different story. Depending where you live and who your friends are, you might not hear very many conversations about religion. And when you do, it's often in the context of politics. As in: "the Christian right," "extremist Muslims," or "fundamentalists" of any stripe.

You hear people arguing, you hear people getting on their soapboxes, you hear people saying, "We're right and they're wrong." Rarely do you hear a civil conversation about religion. You might get the idea there is no such thing as calm, thoughtful, respectful people who take religion seriously.

When I was in high school, no one ever told me not to talk about religion. They didn't have to. I could tell from observing and listening to my peers that no one wanted to go there. That it would be completely weird and uncool to be sitting around the lunch table and suddenly bow my head to pray over my cafeteria

spaghetti ("Dear Lord, please don't let me get food poisoning...").
On Mondays, when my friends and I talked about our weekends,
I never mentioned anything about Sunday mornings at church,
even though church and the people in it were a big part of my life.

There just seemed to be this unspoken rule: *don't do that.*

So I developed a kind of split personality. One side of me cared
deeply about trying to understand who God is and what my faith
meant about the best way I should live. The other side of me cared
deeply about not being a social outcast.

I put away the religious part of me for the school day and
brought it out for air on Sundays and sometimes during the week
if the nonreligious side of me wasn't too busy with homework and
obsessing about boys.

This worked for awhile. But as I got into my twenties and
went to college, my divided self started to mess with me. Who
was I, *really*? Sometimes I thought maybe the nonreligious part of
me was more real. Maybe I didn't really believe what I thought I
believed. Other times I was very sure about my religious identity,
yet I still hid that part of myself from certain groups of friends.

As a result, I felt like no one truly knew me. My religious
friends didn't know the side of me that liked to have fun and tell
edgy jokes and rock out to Van Halen. My nonreligious friends
didn't know what I thought about God, the meaning of life, and
my purpose in it.

It's kind of a terrible thing to feel like no one knows you, that
you're never being 100 percent *you.*

I started to gradually try to integrate these two parts of myself.
How did I do this? Well, for one, I started to talk about activities
around my faith, such as going to church, without embarrassment.
Also, whenever someone from my faith said something publicly
that was mean, crazy, or just plain wrong, I spoke up to my friends
so that they wouldn't have to wonder, *Does Sara secretly agree with
that TV preacher who says this natural disaster is God's punishment
of certain people?* (No, she doesn't!)

When I became a published author, I knew that part of it involved being a public person. I decided early on, before anyone ever heard about me, that I would be 100 percent open about my faith. I would be 100 percent wicked sense of humor, rock-loving, God-doubting me *and* 100 percent true believer. The divided parts of me called a truce, reunited, and it feels so good.

Now, to some rule breaking.

If you're not religious, you might believe that all religious people are nuts, or only practice religion because they're old and close to death and therefore clinging to anything and everything. You've somehow learned and believed in a rule that makes you tune out whenever religion comes up. Which may seem like no big deal, but there are a couple of problems with this.

First, you're missing out on the full range of the cultural conversation about faith, which has shaped world history for millennia! Nearly all major world events are somehow tied into religion and religious differences. Take the time to find out how religion is affecting your world today.

Second, and more important, you may be missing out on *really* knowing some of your friends. Try to be open to friends that may take some kind of religious faith seriously. If you don't understand or are curious about something that has to do with their religious practice, ask! Take the time to get to know what they believe. There's nothing to be afraid of, and it will make your friendship so much deeper.

If you *are* religious, you might decide to go into hiding with your faith because it only seems to lead to arguments, plus maybe you are constantly mortified by the things that other people of your faith say and do. Then *you're* missing out on the full experience of your religion, and denying part of your identity. Which is never good. Think about what it costs you to live a double life, and if it's a price you're willing to pay.

When you talk about religion with friends who don't share your faith, don't get defensive. No one's words or opinions can take your faith away from you. And, I believe that no matter what your Sunday school teacher told you in fifth grade, you shouldn't try to convert your friends. The best way you can share your faith is by living it sincerely and openly and by being the best friend you can be.

There. I talked about religion. That wasn't so bad, was it?

FOLLOW THE MONEY, NOT YOUR HEART

LISA SCHROEDER

"Get a business degree," my mother told me when I was a senior in high school and trying to make decisions about college. "You can do lots of things with a business degree. There's money in business."

And so I did. I went to Oregon State University, majored in business, and worked in the field of human resources for a number of years.

My mom, bless her heart, wanted me to be able to support myself, and support myself well. I know that. As a single mother, she had gone back to school in her thirties—not an easy thing to do. She had struggled at times to make ends meet, and she didn't want the same for me.

It's not that I couldn't do the work I chose. I did it, and I did it pretty well. But it didn't make my heart sing. It was simply a means to an end—a way to pay the bills. What I've come to learn is that we spend a huge amount of our time at work to pay those silly bills, and it's really best if we can find work that we're passionate about.

The trouble is, when we're young, we don't know what that passion might be. Or if we do, family members who care about us and have more life experience than we do often worry that passions such as music or writing or art or horses or any number of things don't necessarily make good careers.

When I was a teen, I loved to sing. My freshman year, I took choir (it was offered as an elective class). My teacher chose me to compete in the state's solo competition. As a freshman, it was more for practice than anything, but I received fairly good marks and my teacher wanted me to participate the following year.

But there are only so many electives to go around. At the advice of family members, I took accounting and typing and dropped out of choir my sophomore year. That is where my journey began, away from subjects that made my heart sing and toward more "practical" subjects. I can still remember my choir teacher stopping me in the halls the beginning of sophomore year, telling me how disappointed he was that I hadn't joined again.

I was so confused. Listen to my parents? Listen to my teacher? Had I made the wrong decision, even though I did what caring, loving people had told me to do?

What I should have done is listened to my heart. But that's not always an easy thing to do, especially as a teenager, when so many other people think they know better than you.

I believe that each of us is given a specific gift in life in terms of talents and abilities, sometimes more than one, and it's our job to figure out what that gift may be and how to use it. Do you know what you're good at? Do you nurture whatever talents, skills, or abilities you have? If not, you should!

So often in our society we focus on what we're bad at and put lots of energy there. Not good at math? Well then, let's hire you a tutor. We'll make you spend even more time on math than you usually do because, dang it, math is important.

But, wait a second. I would say math is important for *some* people, but not for everyone. If math isn't your strength, if math is something you despise with every fiber of your being, do you really think you'll end up doing something where lots and lots of math is required? Probably not. (But please don't drop out of math. A certain number of math credits are required for graduation. So, take math. And do your best.)

Now, let's say you are an amazing artist. You love to draw and spend lots of your spare time with a sketch pad. Are you nurturing this talent? Taking art classes? Learning about art and how to become better at your craft? I hope so.

When I started writing 10 or so years ago, alongside my day job, I knew how hard it was to get published. I'd heard it was almost impossible, in fact. But still, I had this tiny sliver of hope that maybe, someday, if I worked hard enough, I might be able to make a career out of being an author for kids and teens. I didn't tell anyone that, though. I just wrote story after story and learned as much about the publishing business as I could while I continued to work and raise my family.

Eventually, after years and years of writing, I sold one book. Then another book. And then another one. It took a long time, but I was finally able to break away from a human resources career and make a living doing something I love.

When a well-meaning adult asks you why you're taking a class or why you're pursuing a certain career or any number of things, don't be afraid to say, "Because it's what I love to do."

Have you ever heard the saying, "Do what you love and the money will follow"? I'm a big believer in this. But sometimes, in order to do that which we love, it requires us to take chances or to make sacrifices. And people who care about us often don't want us to take chances or to make sacrifices, because they are afraid for us.

I'd argue, however, it's not a good idea to use fear as the guide for your life. Love and joy, those are good emotions to use as your guide. So don't do what I did. Break the rules! Tell your parents or grandparents or teachers or whomever it is that it's important for you to follow the path you are most passionate about. Follow the path of your heart, and then see what happens.

After all, you can change paths at any time, just like I did, along with so many other people who were lawyers, teachers, accountants, and a hundred other things before they became authors.

Follow your heart. And most of all, enjoy the journey.

LOOK LIKE A MAGAZINE COVER

SAYANTANI DASGUPTA

Boys and girls, children of all sizes, races, shapes and ages—step right up! Step right up into our carnival of funhouse mirrors. Want to feel bad about your weight, shape, or size? We have an image for that! Want to feel bad about your skin color, hair, nose, zits, butt? We have an image for that too! Whatever your self-loathing needs, we have it! Stress? Treat yo'self! Low self-esteem? Treat yo'self! Disordered eating? Treat yo'self!

So I have a dirty little secret.

And because I don't know you at all, I'll tell you.

I am addicted to images.

Images on billboards, images in magazines, images on the sides of moving buses, images on TV and in movies. Like a moth to a flame, I naturally gravitate to the colors and shapes in ads and advertisements: images of clothes and handbags, of jewelry and shoes, images of beautiful people doing made-up things like drinking fake drinks and laughing at silent jokes. I'm addicted to images of unrealistic situations, like handsome men and women wearing birdcages as hats, or a group of pretty people hanging out in a bathtub on top of a mountain, or models slouching around the desert inexplicably oblivious to the pack of growling pumas closing in on their bad-postured party.

Like a smoker, an alcoholic, like an addict of any kind, I'm endlessly drawn to these images even though I know they're bad for me, bad for all of us. And I'm not the only one. (Fellow secret watchers of *America's Next Top Model*, I think you know what I'm talking about. Yes, I'm looking at you. And no, learning about "smizing" or the "booty tooch" does not actually qualify as an educational activity.)

> *Ads sell more than products. They sell values, they sell images, they sell concepts of love and sexuality, of success, and perhaps most important, of normalcy. They tell us who we are and what we should be.*
> **—Jean Kilbourne,** Killing Us Softly video series

Images in the media are designed to impact us—emotionally, intellectually, consciously, and subconsciously. More than ever before in history, we're bombarded by these images—from hundreds of television channels, from the Internet, from our phones, and other handheld devices, from music videos and social media platforms.

Yet, when I was a teenager, half these things hadn't even been invented yet. (There was life before *ANTM*! A time before the interwebz! Shocking to contemplate, but true.) Still, the power of such images in my life was clear. I loved the eye candy—the beauty and desirability I saw all around me.

But in turn, I hated myself.

When I was a teenager, I was convinced I was intolerably ugly. Everywhere I looked, there were faces and bodies I thought I was supposed to aspire to. Yet those faces and bodies looked nothing like mine. What I saw around me was blonde, tall, thin, sexy haired, and pouty mouthed. Nowhere was someone who looked like me—brown skinned, dark haired, short(ish).

That inability to see myself in the environment around me lent to me the sense that I was hideous, socially unappealing, unacceptable. I developed a sharp sense of humor and would laugh off compliments—convinced that the person giving me the compliment was teasing me or, worse, administering some kind of sick psychological test (She's not really going to fall for thinking she's pretty, is she?). This inability to see myself in my world convinced me—subconsciously—that maybe I *should* be invisible, or that just maybe I didn't have the right to live in the world at all.

And so I hid. Not actually, but in various, metaphorical ways at various points of my life: behind humor, behind shyness, behind a swath of pulled-down hair, behind a self-defeating attitude, behind my beloved books and stories, behind others, behind fear, behind a lack of confidence. Like the kid I used to babysit who would throw a kitchen towel over his face during hide and seek and think that I couldn't see him, it wasn't particularly effective. But it was painful.

I had a group of close friends, but even they, I sometimes worried, were simply humoring me, or putting up with me. I was terrified to use my body, to claim my voice, to take up space. As if I were a rabbit frozen in the path of the wolf, there was a part of my heart that froze up too: the part tasked with loving myself. And it took me years to defrost it.

I'm not blaming images alone. Clearly, media is both the message and the messenger. It constructs images of beauty and desirability while reflecting to us society's preexisting ideals. Sexism, racism, sizeism, you name it: the media doesn't invent these oppressions. But it does participate in perpetuating them. Consider race: despite the presence of many more people of color in the public eye now than when I was young, the fact remains that lighter hues are still considered more attractive. We only have to look to the spate of "whitewashing" on magazine and book covers—darker skinned people being made to look lighter skinned or lighter haired—to see that this clearly holds true. Recent controversies around American singer Beyoncé or Indian model and actress Aishwarya Rai Bachchan being portrayed on magazine covers as lighter skinned and haired than they are in real life are cases in point.

> *Too many black and Asian children grow up understanding the sad truth that to have dark skin is to be somehow inferior.... When black celebrities appear to deny their heritage by trying to make themselves look white, I despair for the youngsters who see those images.*
>
> **—Yasmin Alibhai-Brown**

Or consider size. Despite the new movement, Health at Every Size (HAES), and some attempts by the modeling world to represent people of different body types, the truth remains that the media represents unrealistic ideals of thinness, which contributes, of course, to body shame and disordered eating among both men and women. When even svelte celebrities such as Jessica Alba or Eva Mendes are airbrushed and Photoshopped to look smaller waisted, bigger busted, and overall thinner, what hope is there for the rest of us out there?

Even more disastrously, think about the passive, disembodied, highly sexualized ways that women are portrayed in advertising, music videos, or television. Media critics such as Jean Kilbourne, responsible for the Killing Us Softly video series, has shown time and again how women's and girls's bodies are used in advertising in ways that promote a culture of violence against us in real life. Or forget those gyrating, dominated, splayed-open images of women in ads and videos. Just think about the ways that real-life, powerful women are reduced to their body parts. The news media's focus on

Hillary Clinton's hairstyles or Sarah Palin's bustline only serves to locate all women's worth on their bodies to the exclusion of their brains. And this is as bad for girls and women—and the way we think about ourselves—as it is for boys and men, and the way they think about themselves in relation to their mothers, partners, sisters, colleagues, bosses, and friends.

> *If a woman is looked upon as an object, without feelings, life, soul, or thoughts, then it is easy to ingest images of her that defy her humanity. She is not a woman—a living creature with human attributes. She is merely a body, a vacant, empty, vessel intended to contain the needs of others— preferably men—and her body, which is the most desired aspect of her existence, perfect, lithe, smooth, and hair-free, is open for interpretation and domination.*
> **—Marina DelVecchio**

Why does the media do all this? Well, it's not evil. Not inherently, anyway. The job of not just the advertising media but, increasingly, all other forms of media (including music, television, movies, and so on) is to support the profits of the businesses that bankroll them. Media creates a psychological need in us as viewers that convinces us we want to emulate those we see, or, more concretely, that we want to buy a fix for whatever's wrong with us so that we can approximate the lives of those we see. And if that involves feeling bad about ourselves, so be it.

Frizzy hair? We have a product for that. Chin zit? We have a product for that. Bad breath? We have a product for that too. Even problems we didn't realize we had now have solutions—from thin eyelashes to ugly armpits!

> *One of the secrets of sales is fulfilling the public's need. And another is inventing the public's need. I thought we had*

reached the peak of making money off female insecurity until I heard of a breakthrough shame-o-vation ... Women have now heard that their armpits are hideous. Why sell women products for a need they already have? If you invent a new thing for women to feel insecure about, then sell them the solution, you've cornered the market.

— **Stephen Colbert,** *The Colbert Report*

So what do we do about it? Well, Maine eighth grader Julia Bluhm had one solution. In 2012, she circulated a petition asking *Seventeen* magazine to stop Photoshopping and airbrushing images of models, arguing that photographs of perfect skin, hair, and rail-thin bodies were unhealthy for young people's self-esteem. Her petition gained national media attention and even inspired a protest in front of *Seventeen*'s offices. After months of being ignored by the magazine, it seems she might have recently gotten a positive reaction, being mentioned by the editor-in-chief in her monthly editorial. Yet, the long-term commitment of the magazine to avoid Photoshopping models remains to be seen.

Others, from the American Medical Association to pro-healthy body image websites such as Adios, Barbie agree to this ban on Photoshopping. At the very least, many have suggested that such images come with warning labels such as: "Warning: This image is a digital interpretation," or "Warning: This image has been retouched to distort your idea of perfection," or even "Warning: *Do not read* or open this magazine because it will, I repeat, it will lower your self esteem (if you let it ...) and raise unknown insecurities. It is hazardous to your health. *Open at your own risk!!!*"

Activists such as Julia Bluhm, critics such as Jean Kilbourne, and organizations such as Adios, Barbie are all a part of the body-loving revolution—a revolution dedicated to finding ways to use media to promote self-worth and self-esteem.

*The media can be an instrument of change. It can maintain
the status quo and reflect the views of the society or it can
awaken people and change minds. It depends on who's
piloting the plane.*
　　　　　　　—Katie Couric, *Miss Representation*

So I guess what I want to share with you is the lesson I learned
the hard way: don't try to look like a magazine cover. You can't
anyway. (Even the people on the magazine covers don't look like
that!) Instead, add your own voice to the voices already raised in
protest against the tyranny of such images. Let's use media in
ways to promote us all, rather than break us all down. Let's grab
the controls and pilot this plane.

Gorgeous the way you are? Treat yo'self! Unbowed by convention? Treat yo'self! Smart and strong? Treat yo'self!

I end here with the words of the most fabulous comedienne
Margaret Cho, who reminds us,

*You know when you look in the mirror and you think, "Oh
I'm so fat, I'm so old, I'm so ugly?" Don't you know that's not
your authentic self, but that is billions upon billions of dollars
of advertising, magazines, movies, billboards all geared to
make you feel s**** about yourself so you will take your hard-
earned money and spend it at the mall on some turnaround
cream that doesn't turn around s***? When you don't have
self-esteem, you will hesitate before you do anything in your
life. You will hesitate to go for the job you really want to go
for, you will hesitate to ask for a raise, you will hesitate to call
yourself an American, you will hesitate to report a rape, you
will hesitate to defend yourself when you are discriminated
against for your race, your sexuality, your size, your gender.
You will hesitate to vote, you will hesitate to dream. For us to
have self-esteem is truly a revolution. And our revolution is
long overdue.*

May I repeat, boy and girls: For us to have self-esteem is truly a revolution. And our revolution is long (long!) overdue.

* * * * *

Want to learn more, or add your own voice to the body-loving revolution? Here are some resources to check out:

1. Jean Kilbourne's Killing Us Softly video series on advertising and women: www.jeankilbourne.com/videos/
2. *Miss Representation*, a documentary on media and women: www.missrepresentation.org/
3. The body-positive website Adios, Barbie: www.adiosbarbie .com
4. Stephen Colbert's "Buy and Cellulite": www.colbertnation .com/the-colbert-report-videos/381642/april-13-2011/the -word-buy-and-cellulite
5. Margaret Cho's "Our Revolution is Long Overdue": www .youtube.com/watch?v=I4XP7KvIecI

DON'T TELL LIES

LESLIE CONNOR

The first thing I should tell you is that—*gulp*—I actually sort of *like* rules. Well, some of them. Here are a few of my favorites:

No spitting.

Wait your turn in line.

Don't interrupt when someone else is speaking.

And these:

No biting.

Don't drink and drive. (I love this rule. Please, always, always, always follow this rule.)

And these:

Don't litter.

Do reuse.

Do recycle.

I like the rules that encourage us to be courteous to each other, the ones that keep our bodies and hearts from being broken, and the ones that protect our planet. These are no-brainer rules for me, the ones I can't imagine anyone arguing with. But there are times when the question of what's right or wrong gets fuzzier. That's when I think it's a relief to have rules that get everybody on the same page and let everyone know what is expected. I *want* to know what the rules are in any given setting, even if I don't agree with them all. I get very embarrassed if I break a rule that I didn't even know about. Yikes!

I think of it this way: a rule is a decision that I've been asked to make. Remember the no biting rule? Well, in those moments when I very much wanted to *bite* my brother I knew that my parents wanted me to *decide* not to. (It's been a really long time since I've wanted to bite my brother but for the record, it would have been all about something *he* started.)

Like everybody else, I go up against rules all the time—even the ones I *like*. I become conflicted, or one of my passions takes hold of me. I have broken rules. I have interrupted others; that's what it is to be bursting with an idea. I'm curious and I like adventuring and testing my own limits. But I don't want my day ruined with a trip to the ER either. Sometimes a rule reminds me to be cautious. (I must not have been thinking of that when I did all those cartwheels off the diving board at the YMCA when the lifeguard wasn't looking. Oh, it was so much fun ... but I *was* breaking a rule.)

Here are some rules I *don't* like:

Keep your chairs in straight rows. (I like chairs in horseshoes and huddles.)

No dogs on the bed. (Guess what happens at my house?)

Never tell a lie.

Yep, you heard that last one right. I *like* lying. I'm a lifetime liar. A career liar, really, because as a fiction writer, that's what I do all day—I tell lies. I had some practice at this as a kid. I didn't tell the kind of lies that really hurt anyone. In fact, sometimes I lied to try to protect the people I cared about. But I told plenty of lies that made people mad too. I didn't plan my lies. I would suddenly find myself in the middle of them. When I was very little, I think I didn't really know the difference between truth and lies. But later on, I did know better, and it caused me some trouble with my friends, believe me. Yet all that invention and exaggeration came so naturally to me it sometimes seemed magical, and I found I just couldn't give it up.

I think I must have been very hungry for stories. My own life wasn't interesting or exciting enough. So there I went, dressing up the truth, and tossing in all sorts of things that came from inside my head. The trouble was, my society—the society of elementary school—had one of those understood, if unwritten, rules that said:

Don't tell lies.

I laugh as I write this because I wasn't the only person I knew who was struggling to stick to one kind of rule or another during elementary school. I remember a boy in my grade who could *not* stop speaking out during class. He broke that rule about six times every morning, and he did it *for years.* I couldn't help feeling bad for him as he packed up his papers and headed to the principal's office time and time again. His outbursts were distracting and tiresome but he wasn't really a *bad* kid.

Then there was that girl who sat at a desk right next to mine. She hummed while she worked, and that humming seemed to wind all the way through her until it blossomed into song. She danced her fingers across the top of her desk. She tapped and shuffled her feet until her chair rocked. When she stood in line with our class in the hallway she bounced up and down like a Slinky. Outburst Boy and Slinky Girl both annoyed me, just like I annoyed the people around me with my ridiculous yarns about famous-artist uncles, goldfish in the family swimming pool (yes, really), and mystifying ancestral cases of influenza involving the highest fevers ever seen by doctors. Looking back, I think that all three of us, the outburster, the chair rocker, and the liar, might well have been doing exactly what each of us was born to do. But it wasn't working very well for any of us. Not yet.

But by high school, the boy who shouted out in class was using that big voice to announce basketball games. He now has a job that requires him to give presentations to large audiences every week.

What about the bouncing, tapping, singing girl? She performed a lively solo at a junior high school concert. She was the lead in at least one of our high school musicals, and she studied ballet in college.

Then there was me. Remember, I still had a head full of lies and a deep longing for story. I knew I wasn't going to find anyone who was dying to sit down and listen to me spin a whopper. So in my case, I learned to tell it to the page. At first it wasn't so satisfying. I missed the reactions, for sure—the wide eyes, the looks of awe and (ahem) *disbelief.* But I also felt freer than ever. My new place to lie was a much safer place to lie. It wasn't even lying any more. It was writing. Phew! So much more acceptable! It was easier, too, to let those tales roar without the confines of real life and real people. I not only wrote stories, I drew them. In fact, sometimes I drew more than I wrote. I kept art and writing journals going constantly, one after the other. Whenever anyone asked me what I was doing I could be honest and say, "I'm making stuff up."

Inventing characters was like inventing a new skin to slip myself into—a permissible way to have a slice of that more exciting life I was so busy chasing. I also started to watch life more, and by that I mean that I took more of an eyes-wide-open approach to the world. I watched other people and made guesses, right or wrong, as to how they felt about what they were experiencing. Practicing compassion helped me to become a better friend. I understood why people didn't want to be lied to. Now I tell stories in the books I write. It's the same creative energy I always had. I'm still working from real life and adding the drama from my own imagination.

We go through changes all our lives, but to some degree I think that even in elementary school we are who we are. (Or, at least there is some evidence there of who we will become.) So how can you be yourself and still be accepted if you are a little quirky and just a little bit prone to breaking rules? Well, maybe the first thing you need is a list of "Rules for Breaking the Rules." Here's an important one: Be appropriate.

It comes back to deciding, really—deciding when it's a good time and place to shout out, or sing and bounce up and down, or conjure tales. If you want to break a rule make sure it's going to really work for you. This is the part that takes time to learn. So relax and be comforted. You've probably heard the phrase, "practicing the rules." Practicing means you should have *at least* a few years to get it right.

The rule you are aching to break could be a key to your greatest strength and to the big gift you're going to share with this world. The "worst" thing about you might really be the best thing, and I swear, I'm not lying.

PRETEND THE DARK STUFF ISN'T TRUE

CAROL LYNCH WILLIAMS

It's true.

I was always the obedient one. From the moment I was born, no matter what would happen, I would be obedient. Bend-over-backward-I'm-sorry-I-didn't-do-better-I-swear-to-do-more obedient.

As a young girl I did the laundry, paid the bills for my mother, kept the house clean, and, sometimes, cooked.

As I got older I gave every single paycheck I made to my mom so she could meet the bills. I worried about finances. I worried that the cars wouldn't start. I worried, even, about the older neighbors.

My sister was a different story.

She did whatever, whenever, however she wanted. She was smoking by the age of 10, moved out at 15, decided to be a nurse and put herself through school—living on her own mind you—by the time she was 20. She was the black sheep.

I was the good girl.

And I ... I was broken.

But obedient to a fault.

Can you be too good?

In tough situations that might keep you alive, you gotta do what's right. Like, you don't want to run the stop sign, right? And you didn't want to cross my mom.

Ever. Because if you did … Well, parts of that story, my life story, you can find in bits and pieces of my novels.

*   *   *   *   *

But when I wrote … when I wrote my characters were drunks, killer puppeteers, and crazy people.

My first writing that I remember was a play for two characters. My sister and I performed this play for our grandmother, Nana. I couldn't have been more than six. It was about a drunken man who sat at a bar and imagined a beautiful girl dancing around (in my grandmother's shortie nightgown) singing, "One more for the road, big boy."

Where did that come from?

I'm still not sure. I've never even sat at a bar except when I've been with my editors (no, I'm not trying to drown my editorial sorrows) in New York.

*   *   *   *   *

My mother always wanted to publish. She and I wrote screenplays together (we never sold anything), read the same books, and went to every play the local college put on. The one thing Mom did right in my life was tell me I was a natural writer.

By the time I was 16, I was writing furiously. Funny stuff. About two naughty sisters who peed in the middle of the road and fussed over their irreverent grandfather who was a terrible example to all who lived on Adeline Street. Those stories ended up in my first book, *Kelly and Me.* There were dead dogs, crazy neighbors, car wrecks, and, of course, the pee.

That book hadn't been on the shelves long when a neighbor who lived across the street from me said, "I'll not let my children read your books."

I was surprised. We were standing outside, and I remember the sun was in my eyes.

"OK," I said. She wanted me to ask, "Why not?"

Ever obedient, I asked.

"Because the children are too naughty," she said.

I just looked at her. "You think the characters in a book will make your kids act badly? Really?"

She did.

Perhaps she wasn't as good a parent as she thought if she worried a middle grade novel would make her children run peeing into the middle of the road.

I wonder if her kids, who have kids of their own now, read.

*   *   *   *   *

People ask me quite often about why my characters face such challenges. The writer part of me wants to say it makes for a better story. Gives you a bit of a plot. Gives your characters the chance to grow and become different by the end of the book.

But it's more than that.

As I look back in my writing life, I can see that I've had several characters who rebelled against controlling adults. Twelve-year-old Caitlynne in *The True Colors of Caitlynne Jackson* confronts her physically abusive mother, knowing by the end of the novel that she is strong enough to take care of herself, if she must. Almost-14-year-old Kyra stands up to the leaders of her community in *The Chosen One* when she has to marry someone much older than she is, someone she doesn't love. Hope, who is 13, does what she can to protect her older sister from her mom by speaking out to people who can help in *Glimpse*. Lacey, another 13-year-old, takes care of her mentally ill mother but finally looks to taking care of herself when she realizes she must in *Miles from Ordinary*.

* * * * *

So, I know someone else who hates that I write these kinds of books.

"We don't need dark books," she says. "We don't need stories where kids rebel, where parents are bad. We need happy stories. There's too much darkness in the world as it is. Why add to it?" She ends her argument with, "And I'm sick of people saying that readers need examples of kids surviving tough situations."

Isn't that exactly who needs books? If life were always rosy, always perfect, never flawed—if we never had troubles, never needed comfort—well, why read?

For me, dark stories are intimate. Readers recognize themselves in the characters of books and feel like they have a chance. Just recently a grown woman said to me, "Knowing that Caitlynne stood up to abuse and said 'no more' gave me the courage to say 'no more' to my almost-adult child who was abusing me."

I do want readers (no matter their age) to have examples of survivors. I do want to write and speak for the person who has no words. I do want to show the darkness and then the strength it takes to rebel when necessary. I do want to show what I feel is truth.

I want to decide if I can or can't. I want to keep my individual freedom. I want to read the books I want to read and I want to write the books I want to write, dark and rebellious and sometimes heartbreakingly ugly.

* * * * *

The truth is, we each want to be able to choose. We want to make decisions for ourselves. I think it's a natural instinct. As soon as someone says "You have no choice," I can feel every part of my being rebelling against those words. Maybe I shouldn't admit this, but when I see the road signs that say, RIGHT LANE MUST TURN, I have to squelch the voice inside that says, *Oh yeah? We'll see about that!*

That voice that fights for our own freedom, though, is good in the right circumstances. It gives us the courage to stand up to those who are unfair, it gives us the courage to stand up for ourselves, it helps us tell the truth or fight or remain stubborn.

Not too long ago I was in the local grocery store with my oldest daughter, Elise. For some reason, my eyes and ears are trained to spot abuse and, sure enough, in the bread section of the store I saw a father hurting his little boy—a child small enough to take a pacifier.

I yelled across the store for the abusive father to stop what he was doing. He and his wife and children quickly left the store, Elise and me following at a brisk pace (I was going to get his license plate number). The father, however, turned and ran at Elise and me, threatening us with his words, saying he would teach us a lesson. My daughter stepped between me and this man, ready to fight him if necessary.

I can't say that the reason she did this was because I have always encouraged her to stick up for the innocent, those who have no voice, or because I have encouraged her to read the books that might make her feel a bit uncomfortable. It was something more than that—the part of Elise that makes her believe everyone deserves something good in life—including the ability to choose.

*   *   *   *   *

Books give that to readers. Especially those edgy books that push the envelope and make the reader say, "Yes, I'm worth it."

DON'T DAYDREAM

WENDY MASS

The flat, rectangular stone inside my new ring was purple indoors, and green outdoors. And it wasn't one of those cheap mood rings from the mall that everyone knows just change color based on body temperature. This was the real deal—an amethyst, set in a delicate gold band and delivered to me by my parents the night I turned 13. They'd had it for years, they explained, waiting until they thought I'd be old enough to care for it properly.

I loved that ring. But not because it was pretty, although it was. And not because it marked a new level of trust and responsibility within my family's hierarchy. I loved it because when I sat in class and tilted it to the side ever so slightly, I could see a whole other world in the face of the purple stone.

The first time it happened was accidental. I was taking notes in my notebook and out of the corner of my eye, the image of a house suddenly appeared in my ring. I remember gasping, shocked. I tilted my hand to the right, and the house disappeared. No! I quickly tilted it back. The house returned. Tilting to the left brought more houses and lawns and a road. I honestly, for about a full minute, thought I was glimpsing another world, purple and full of fairy-tale creatures and lawns that sprouted only purple grass. My heart pounded with excitement. I'm sure I didn't hear a thing the teacher said.

I had a magic ring!

And then … well, a car drove by. *Inside the ring.* That broke the spell. It finally occurred to me to look outside the window, two rows away from my desk. There were the houses and the lawns and the street. Not purple. Not exotic. Unlikely to be harboring pixies. I was heartbroken. My ring was only a mirror.

On the way out of class my teacher stopped me. "I noticed you were daydreaming a lot today. We have a midterm coming up next week. Is everything all right, you know, at home? With your friends?"

I hesitated, then nodded. How could I explain about finding—and losing—a secret world that lived only inside my ring? That would ensure a trip to the guidance counselor for sure. "Good," my teacher said, already turning away. "Then there's no reason to be daydreaming. Please pay more attention in the future."

That night I tucked the ring back into the box and hoped my parents didn't ask why I wasn't wearing it. The next morning I walked to school past the street I'd glimpsed outside the window. The block looked so plain and ordinary, like reality was somehow dimmed.

In class I paid attention this time, as the teacher had instructed me to. After all, I didn't have problems at home or with my friends, so what excuse did I have to daydream? I took notes. I even asked a question. But I felt a sadness that I couldn't pinpoint. When I left school that day and walked past the street again, I knew what the sadness was about. When I first saw the house in my ring and thought it from some magical land, I had imbued it with a sense of wonder, of mystery. No real house, or real life, could live up to that.

Or could it? I stood there while my friends kept walking. I looked at the house, ordinary in every way. Lawn, front door, mailbox, picket fence. But who's to say what's going on inside? Maybe every brick was brought from some exotic country, and laid down exactly as it had been found, hidden in the woods, or atop a mountain. Or maybe the chimney was a magic portal to some distant and timeless land, like Narnia. (I was big on Narnia back then. Still am!) Maybe sitting inside that mailbox right now was a letter that would change the life of the person who lived there. It took two friends snapping their fingers in my face to bring me out of this daydream.

That night, I put the ring back on. I went through my house, tilting my hand as I went, watching things from a slant. What I found when I looked up was that I could see the objects I had seen in the ring differently. A little bit of the magic had leaked out from inside the ring. My surroundings felt a little more special. I realized for the first time how much our imagination—allowed to roam free in our daydreams—can transform the ordinary into the extraordinary. But it can do so much more than that. It can give you confidence to reach your goals; it can help you work out problems, even keep you out of trouble. It can set you free.

Everyone has heard the phrase "you are what you eat." But you're also what you think about. (Although if that first one is entirely accurate, I'd be a box of Junior Mints right now.) It's definitely true that if you set your mind to something, you have a much better chance of reaching it. Daydreaming allows you to keep your goals firmly within you, it helps you to get comfortable with yourself and your innermost feelings and hopes.

When I decided I wanted to write books, I used to daydream about what my life as a writer would be. Sometimes the fantasies would be very pie-in-the-sky. I'd live on a yacht and scribble in my notebook as the wind ruffled through the pages. Or home would be a castle, where my office would perch atop a high tower. Sometimes I'd have a whole staff answering fan mail while I sipped cold ice tea on a wraparound porch. But most of the time the daydreams would be more realistic and down to earth. I'd picture myself filling notebooks with story ideas. I'd imagine what my desk would look like, and how it would feel to walk into a bookstore and see my books on the shelf. I might have missed a few facts about European history, and I still don't really understand what an isosceles triangle is. But I was imprinting my identity, training my mind to work toward my chosen future, the one that hours of daydreaming had helped me picture so clearly.

As Albert Einstein famously said, "Imagination is more important than knowledge. Knowledge is limited. Imagination encircles the world." I could have imagined myself designing skyscrapers, or making the world's best soufflé, or running the fastest 100-meter dash. But those would have been someone else's dreams. And I am very sure no one could become a world-renowned architect, a famous chef, or a future Olympian without first training themselves to feel like one.

In order to create something, you have to imagine it first. Major corporations such as Google and Apple actually build time into their employees' days for daydreaming. This time to dream is when the ideas hit, when the magic happens, and they don't want to miss it. When your mind wanders, it connects dots that you wouldn't otherwise see. By imagining different scenarios, your subconscious can put the pieces together for you and solve difficult problems that are hard to see when you are staring at them directly.

You can also play out different scenarios in your mind, and pick the best one. Daydreaming allows you to work out problems in a healthy way, by not jumping to conclusions too quickly or responding out of anger. Studies have shown that if a child is engaged in an activity, like building a sand castle, and is imagining a story at the same time, that child will remain engaged much longer than the child who isn't daydreaming as he builds. If the child is busy trying to figure out how his sand crab can rescue the seaweed princess trapped in a tower of shells, he is less likely to become bored and knock over another kid's castle. You don't want to be the kid who knocks over another kid's castle.

When you daydream, you might be alone, but you are never lonely. If you are sad, you can visit a happy memory. If you are hurt, you can visualize yourself healed. The more control you have over your own thoughts, the easier it will be to navigate your way through life. As the Buddhist saying goes, "With our thoughts, we make our world." So the next time a teacher tells you to stop daydreaming, you should probably listen.

But only for a little while.

After all, you've got important work to do.

GO TO COLLEGE AFTER HIGH SCHOOL

CHRIS BARTON

I went to college right after high school, so know that when I tell you to break that rule, I'm telling you to break a rule that I didn't break myself. If you think that vaporizes any credibility I might have on the matter, by all means, move on to other essays in this book. If you're still willing to give me the benefit of the doubt, though, stick around and I'll tell you about the blueberries.

Still here? OK, so—one other thing. I enjoyed college. Some of my best friends all these years later are people I met there. I wouldn't have the children that I do if I hadn't met their mom in college. And I have no regrets about the trajectory that college-after-high-school put me on, since I love the life I have today as a result. Again, then: credibility check! If you think I've just lost any credibility that I might still have had, I understand, and I appreciate you reading this far—enjoy the rest of the book. Everyone else, it's your last chance to bail before enduring a fruit anecdote, because I swear I'm about to get to the blueberries.

All right, then. Blueberries.

By the time I graduated from high school, I already knew I wanted to write for a living. I didn't have much planned for my last summer in my small hometown before I went off to the University of Texas—and, more important, began writing for the college newspaper, the *Daily Texan*. So, you would think that, back in the preblog days, when an area newspaper offered me a story assignment and the chance to connect with readers numbering in the double or maybe even triple digits, I would have been all over it.

But the story was about a local blueberry farm. Blueberries? I liked them in muffins and pancakes, but I didn't know anything about blueberry farming. Nothing about it had appeared in the pages of my biweekly bible, *Rolling Stone* magazine. I didn't think I could possibly find anything interesting in blueberry farming. I turned down the assignment.

Maybe that strikes you as a perfectly logical decision. It sure made sense to me at the time. But before many years had passed, I came to see that decision not as perfectly logical but as clear evidence that I was not ready for college—not ready, at least, to get as much from the experience as I could have.

I didn't know anything about blueberry farming. That sounds to me today like a terrific opportunity to learn something—every fact I would have encountered about blueberry farming would have been something I did not know before. Given my intended profession, what I needed more than anything else—more than a copyediting class, more than a course on media law and ethics, more than an opportunity to get a lot of my writing published in the *Texan*—was curiosity about the world.

I would have been well served by possession of the sort of curiosity that would make me wonder what went into blueberry farming. The sort of curiosity that would lead me to ask questions and try to understand what kind of person does well in that line of work. The sort of curiosity that, I think, would have also made me question my knee-jerk assumption that college right after high school was the right path for me.

For me.

For me, college reinforced my existing interests. It did not significantly expand them. That quality I needed most—curiosity—did not develop until well after college, and the lack of it contributed to me spending many years creatively adrift during my twenties. For you, college immediately after high school might indeed be the best path. But how can you possibly know that if you don't explore the assumption that it is? And how can you explore that assumption if you exhibit the same blind spot I did when I was your age by not even recognizing it as an assumption but rather accepting it as a given?

Don't expect the adults influencing your life to be much help here. (Maybe they will be, and if so, you're very, very lucky. But don't count on it.) Adults tend not to question the status quo, because that's what they're used to, and it just doesn't occur to them to question it. For a big part of the adult population, the normalcy, the rightness, the *essentialness* of going to college after high school is a major part of that status quo, because that's what they did, or have become convinced that they should have done. And for an outspoken subset of that population—providers of college loans come to mind—you going straight to college is in their best interests.

So you need to figure out for yourself whether going to college after high school—or following any other seemingly obvious path—is an assumption in need of being challenged. And how do you do that? A good way is to try out variations on the statement "I should go to college after high school" and see whether you can come up with some that don't sound so crazy. For example:

"*He* should go to college after high school" might help you see reasons why that path makes sense for one of your friends, which would then allow you to weigh whether those same reasons apply to you.

"I should go to *some nearby city* after high school" might allow you to better understand what you find interesting and appealing about the wider world.

"I should *pursue some activity that doesn't involve 'going' any-where* after high school" might enable you to recognize options in your own backyard that have previously been closed off to you, for whatever reason. What you discover might then be enhanced by college, and vice versa.

"I should go to college *during* high school," just a class here and there—maybe online or through a community college—might totally make sense for you.

For you.

You see, the rule I'm urging you to break isn't "Get a college education" or even "Go to college the fall semester after you graduate from high school." What I'm urging you to do is to determine your own path based not on what your peers are doing or on what our (uncertain, struggling, fearful) society says you *should* do if you don't want a life of uncertainty and struggle and fear, but rather based on your knowledge of yourself, and what *you* need, and what *you're* ready for.

And if you don't know yourself well enough yet to make a decision based on that, might I suggest that you hold off on heading down a path that's going to consume an irreplaceable portion of your life and a considerable amount of money? There's time for college later if that turns out to be the right thing, and there are other options now for getting to know yourself better.

Like working on a blueberry farm. If you give that a try, let me know how it goes. I'm really curious.

BE COOL

KATHRYN ERSKINE

Be who you are and say what you feel, because those who mind don't matter, and those who matter don't mind.
—Theodor Seuss Geisel (Dr. Seuss)

I write this as my 16-year-old relative Tristan lies in a coma after his car accident. It puts life in a suddenly jarring perspective—how precious it is, how short. And how much there is about it that we can't control. But there is also something we can control. What's within us. Who we are. Who we choose to be.

There's a lot of pressure on middle and high school students, especially peer pressure, and I'll bet there always has been. Ask your parents and grandparents. Being cool has been important to every teenager in some fashion probably since caveman days, when Og tried to impress Ogalina by sneaking up on a mammoth and pulling its tail then sprinting away like, well, like a mammoth was after him.

I asked my own kids—one boy and one girl, one in high school and one in middle school—what kind of pressure they felt from their peers. It differed a little between middle and high school. It differed a lot more between girls and boys. There were far more rules for girls to follow to be cool. Boys had only a handful but that meant those rules were more critical; unfortunately, they were also riskier and potentially dangerous.

Any peer rule that doesn't work for you isn't worth following. For example, if it's cool to dis school and not hand in homework or study for tests, what does that do for you? Or not do for you? You're giving up a part of your life for … being cool? Try putting that on your résumé for a job or college. When I was struggling with a high school math class and feeling particularly stupid (not a fun feeling, I know), I was surprised to be complimented by adults for working so hard. But then I thought about it and realized that it was a good thing and something I should be proud of. OK, to be honest, it was a few years after that class before I realized it really was a good thing. It sounds boring, but dedication and discipline—yes, even to classes—proves to others and, more important, to yourself, that you have the tenacity and drive that it takes to be a great football player or musician or business mogul. Now *that's* cool.

Dressing and looking like the cool crowd is often a big source of pressure. What if you don't want to wear the cool clothes or aren't allowed to or can't afford them? Be creative. Make your own style. Here's a secret: if you wear your own style like it's *the* thing to wear, people will actually believe it. It's all in how you carry it off. It's called *chutzpah*. Great word. Even greater concept.

Makeup? Wear it if you want, but don't feel you have to. There are plenty of teenagers out there who are happy with those who don't wear makeup. Hair? Try what you like. A new style or a new color. If it doesn't work out, it'll grow back. Glasses? I remember bemoaning the fact, with some of my ninth grade girlfriends, that we had to wear glasses and boys wouldn't think we were cool. One friend reminded us of a saying, "Boys don't make passes at girls who wear glasses." Our teacher overheard us and said, "Boys who *don't* make passes at girls who wear glasses are simply asses."

Strong language for a teacher, especially one who was also a nun. I don't think I can add anything to that.

Whatever your look, realize it's an expression of you, not actually you, and not something to hide behind. Act like your style is awesome (because it is). You don't have to be stuck up about it, but inside it's OK to be thinking, *They don't know what they're missing,* because you're right. They don't. They think they have to follow all the rules for what's cool. You know that you don't. You have the confidence to be who you are and love yourself for it.

What do you do if you don't want to conform to some or all of the rules to be cool or if the cool group doesn't seem to accept you? No one wants to be an outcast. No one wants to be ridiculed. Most of us want to be part of the group. The critical thing to do is to find, or *make,* your own group. Find the people who appreciate you and who you appreciate, throw in some laughter, and you'll have some good times. How do you find those people? Join a group. It could be a sport, a club, a night class, a social group, a church group, or a volunteer group.

A special word on volunteering, especially if you're having trouble finding the right group or feel that you don't have a friend. School and teenagerhood in general can feel rough, sometimes even like you're in a war zone. You may feel you can do nothing right. So what can you do? Viktor E. Frankl, in *Man's Search for Meaning,* writes of his experience in a concentration camp in World War II. How did he survive? How did he stay human in inhuman conditions? The secret? One secret, at least? Caring for something outside of yourself. You not only do good for others, you also do something very powerful for yourself.

Anne Frank, the Jewish teenager who lived with her family and others in an attic, hiding from Nazis during World War II, had to make do with adult friends, her sister, and a teenage boy. Even as limited as her life was, she expressed herself through her diary. Here's a famous line from that journal: "How wonderful it is that nobody need wait a single moment before starting to improve the world." That's a powerful spirit in the face of dire conditions. If she could do it, I bet you can, too.

And how do you improve the world? By being yourself. Being who you are. Sharing that with the rest of us. One thing we have in common is that we're all unique. That means we all have something valuable to contribute, but being different in middle and high school often isn't valued. Why? People are figuring out who they are and who they're going to be. It's hard to figure that out so while in that transition phase it feels comforting to be—or pretend to be—like everyone else. Change, physical and emotional, is scary, so it's comforting to deny it. And you may be exposed to teasing if you're seen as too unconventional. But denying who you are and who you want to be creates more turmoil inside. Show us the real you.

One particularly powerful exercise teachers do is to have everyone in class write one nice thing on a slip of paper about each student in the room. You've been sitting with these kids all year and you finally hear, *I love that poem she wrote last semester. She's always kind. I like how he holds the door open for people. He's got a great smile and he's not afraid to use it.* Why does it work? Because it's anonymous. We don't want to put ourselves out there, scared of the repercussions. Teachers know that and that's why they do it, hoping that seeing all these positive statements and good feelings will spread not only a little joy and confidence but the idea that it's OK to say these things—we're all thinking them so why not share them?

The reason adults remember that exercise so vividly is that they did feel that no one liked them, everyone was making fun of them, they were being judged by everyone they met. Since most teenagers are busy worrying about what others are thinking, how much time do they really have to pick you apart? Not as much as you'd think. Probably not a lot of time is being wasted on judging you. And even if it were, it would indeed be a waste of time, and it's their time, not yours. You have better things to do with your life. Like being you.

My relative Tristan has now passed away, his organs have been donated to give others life. I could tell you about Tristan and what he loved, who he loved, all those who loved him, what made him laugh, what made him cry, what motivated him, what moved him. But this isn't Tristan's story. It's yours. You're here, and you have the power to be who you want to be. Starting today, starting now. You don't need to wait a single moment. Be the person you want to be for Tristan and all the other teenagers who couldn't. Do it for all the people you love and who love you. But most of all, be the person you want to be for *you*.

SEE YOURSELF THROUGH THE EYES OF OTHERS

JENNIFER REYNOLDS

My freshman year of high school was an especially traumatic one for my self-image. Besides the initiation into a new school and the pressures to make friends, keep friends, and get good grades, there was the ever-present pressure to fit into a specific mold (both literally and figuratively). Flipping through the pages of an old journal I kept in high school, I recently spotted a couple of entries that startled me now that I am a 31-year-old wife, mother, and PhD student researching human trafficking. But back *then*, this is what I felt:

I found out this guy I used to know said something about me, maybe it isn't true but it sounds like him. I guess he said (yes him, the all "macho" one) that I was indeed "gross" . . .

Guess what? So and so and his posse (who I don't know!) were calling me a chessboard. I don't think I'm flat, flat—I know I'm small but that's not flat. It doesn't really bother me because I don't really like him and he says bad things about a lot of people. Just as long as the boy's locker room isn't making fun of my "chessboard" chest, I'll be okay.

Those comments *did* bother me; I know I cried about it. I had never, to my knowledge, done or said anything about the people who lashed out against the way I looked. I was already insecure about various aspects of my body, and every comment (this was definitely not the first or last time I was insulted in this department) contributed to the growing insecurity.

Junior high and high school feel like impossibly difficult years. It's rare to escape without getting teased. But the most disturbing part about rereading these old thoughts and events is that I began believing them to be true. I refused to fully deal with the anger, hurt, and embarrassment I felt. Inside I crumbled and turned the insults into criticism of myself. *If only I looked prettier. If only I were more outgoing. If only they could see me for who I really am.* The truth is that as the insults came and went I ingested their messages and started to hate more and more characteristics about myself. After I admitted to being called a chessboard behind my back, I continued to write:

> *I think that's rude though, commenting on something like that. I don't think anyone should be judged by their chest size (girls). Also, I have pretty bad acne now. I hate it so much! I hate how I look right now—zits, non-healthy looking hair, small chest, tons of freckles on my back and a curved stomach. My hips have gotten huge!*

My voice had been taken over by negativity and insulting comments that told me I was ugly, cheap, and not worth pursuing. The worst remarks to me were the ones that were spoken randomly. If I hadn't provoked it, then for some reason it had more authority; a person wasn't saying anything out of anger, therefore it must truly be what that person saw and thought of me.

These time periods (when inclusion and popularity are held up as extremely desirable) train us to think *first* of others' perceptions of us, and *then* to think of our perceptions of ourselves through their lens. One of my favorite passages of all time was written by

Marianne Williamson and used in a speech by Nelson Mandela. These words give me permission and freedom to pursue what I hold most dear in my heart, and allow me to see the sensibility (rather than absurdity or arrogance) involved in the expedition.

> *Our deepest fear is not that we are inadequate. Our deepest fear is that we are powerful beyond measure. It is our light, not our darkness that most frightens us. We ask ourselves, Who am I to be brilliant, gorgeous, talented, fabulous? Actually, who are you not to be? You are a child of God. Your playing small does not serve the world. There is nothing enlightened about shrinking so that other people won't feel insecure around you … We were born to make manifest the glory of God that is within us. It's not just in some of us; it's in everyone. And as we let our own light shine, we unconsciously give other people permission to do the same. As we are liberated from our own fear, our presence automatically liberates others.*
> —**Marianne Williamson,** *A Return to Love*

I believe the fear that Williamson refers to is partly a result of viewing ourselves through the lens of others' perceptions. They fear the powerful person we could become, and based on their own insecurities, they tease and criticize us to block our paths. By holding another back, they are able to feel an artificial source of power. It can be diagnosed as a virus: they fear they will not be able to survive without dominating another person's actions and thoughts so they work to kill the essence of another.

You do not have to continue to look through the lens of others' bitterness, meanness, or degrading comments. You can learn to trust your own voice, opinion, and vision.

Ever since I was a little girl, I've loved writing. My mother and father still reminisce about a Parents Night they attended when I was in third grade. My teachers had us write a brief note for our parents to read when they came in and sat at our desks. Mine was notoriously pages long, stapled neatly in the upper left-hand corner as add-ons to the paragraph-sized box we each started with. They still laugh at the fact that they felt torn as my teacher started to speak: do they finish their daughter's letter or pay attention up front?

But something happened to my exuberance as I approached high school. This deep desire of mine faded, as I was also influenced by a lack of self-worth. I felt as though I didn't have anything to say that was worthwhile. I was distracted by the voices and opinions of others.

One of my heroes, Mattie Stepanek, reminds me and everyone else about this truth in one of his poems entitled "Heartsong," from his book *Heartsongs*. Mattie was an inspirational 11-year-old child who suffered from a rare form of muscular dystrophy. He set his dreams high and showed the world the power involved in such an endeavor. He was a dreamer, a poet, and a peacemaker. This particular poem reminds us that there is hope, there is love, and there are dreams waiting to become realities deep within each of us. A few striking lines are:

I have a song, deep in my heart,
And only I can hear it.
If I close my eyes and sit very still
It is so easy to listen to my song.
    —Mattie J. T. Stepanek, *Heartsongs*

We often distract ourselves from these "heartsongs" in order to listen to louder, more obnoxious voices that taunt us from outside ourselves. They can lead us in directions we never should have ventured if we were honest with ourselves.

*   *   *   *   *

After I earned a master's degree in communications, my husband and I moved to Flagstaff, Arizona. We were immediately struck by the beauty of the San Francisco Peaks that are the pride of many who live there. Not too long after we settled in, we journeyed the hour and ten minutes to the Grand Canyon. The magnitude and grandeur of this natural wonder is spectacular.

During our visit we commented to each other how the colors, unlike the desert's browns and dull greens, were an elegant mix of reds, pinks, and yellows. The visible layers of the rock served as a metaphor for the life experiences we each held. In high school, I was standing on top of the rocks, but no incisions had been made—no canyon had been formed. There was a river and it was flowing, but I did not see the layers beneath. Throughout the years to the present moment I am slowly allowing the river to cut through the rock of my past experiences. I have faith that in the end that process will reveal magnificent layers that inspire rather than repress and remain buried. It takes time to excavate a past, but it is well worth it.

After the fact, we can't change what has happened. You may not be able to change the voices you have believed any more than I can go back and rewrite my journal entries from high school. But these facts can become historical events; they can become past rather than present. And as you move beyond this pain, you can create extraordinary beauty.

If the Grand Canyon was made up of only one type of rock throughout the ages it would lack the stunning beauty it possesses today. What makes it awe inspiring and a destination for millions of people from all over the world is that a river cut through the rock for miles and miles and miles over many, many years to expose layers of color and texture. It is the history—a glimpse into the past—that is so phenomenal. There is a story that only the Grand Canyon can tell about the ages it has endured, the pain and cutting that has made it the beautiful site it is today.

You, too, have a story to tell about your experiences and how they have created the person you are today. It is the honesty that comes from examining, learning about, and sharing these layers as a whole that is inspirational.

During my life in high school, seeking approval from others was a deeply embedded pattern. It was toxic water to my spirit: I drank it in thinking it was life, but later came to find it was slowly killing me. Our fears, inhibitions, and need for approval from others are our cages. We become so used to hearing these voices and living under their rule that we give away hope of ever overcoming them. They transform into our security. And then we fool ourselves into thinking that our greatest fear is leaving these cages we have created for ourselves, our comfort zone: *What if I fail?* This is a lie that only serves to keep powerful people in captivity.

As Marianne Williamson stated, "Our greatest fear is not that we are inadequate, but that we are powerful beyond measure." *Powerful beyond measure.* What could happen if you allowed yourself to step outside the cages and breathe in the fresh air of your freedom? How could you change the world—even the world of your high school—if you reclaimed your voice and pursued your dreams with reckless abandon? How might you inspire others to do the same, taking the power away from cynical doubters and dream stompers? It *is* worth fighting against the voices that seek to tell you that you can't, you shouldn't, or you aren't worth it.

I am learning to love and appreciate the woman who gazes back at me in the mirror every morning whispering a vote of confidence: *Don't be afraid of the power of your spirit, shine your light bright.* And the voices that taunted me in high school so many years ago? Their strength is hollow, and their message is powerless to touch the real me.

Start now by refusing to see yourself through the lens of others. Others do not define you. Their opinions will not last, and their words hold no power. You define you. And you don't need to fear your strength. It is as captivating as the Grand Canyon itself.

SPEAK UP!

MIKE JUNG

You've heard the old adage, "the squeaky wheel gets the grease," right? I've generally been the wheel that wobbles but doesn't squeak. This has posed some challenges throughout my life, because right now American society inundates us with messages proclaiming the value of high-volume, high-frequency squeaking. We're rabidly encouraged to work the room, speak up, and barrel headlong into confrontation. Raising one's voice has apparently won the race to be our default mode of interaction.

That's never come naturally to me. My mother has often told me the story about her first meeting with my first grade teacher—apparently I was noteworthy for my reticence and would always get my teacher's attention by tapping her on the shoulder and standing there wordlessly until she acknowledged me. This was a sign of things to come.

My cousin Cathy once affectionately described me as "the cousin who was always hidden in a corner with a book," which was an understatement, if anything. On more than one occasion the corner I tucked myself into was in her bedroom, since she had a copious supply of books and was generous about sharing them.

In fourth grade I read an even 100 books (a feat I've yet to duplicate, sadly). Our class had a year long reading competition, with the prize being a sack filled with globules of refined sugar or some equally unhealthy (but competition-inflaming) thing. This contest was great for a spectacularly unathletic, unpopular boy like myself, who often couldn't even see the victory circle at school-based competitions. I read *A Cricket in Times Square, Catcher with a Glass Arm, Tales of a Fourth Grade Nothing, Island of the Blue Dolphins, The Martian Chronicles, The Wind in the Willows,* that goofy Star Wars novel *Splinter of the Mind's Eye,* nonfiction books about sharks and haunted houses, and more. I haunted the public library, walking out with teetering stacks of books in my arms at least once a week.

I was lucky enough to have a friend who was also a voracious reader, and for a time we were in serious competition with each other for the fourth grade book-reading title. In the end I won in a landslide, outpacing my friend by nearly 40 books. It remains one of the proudest achievements of my childhood, and of course it was accomplished almost entirely in silence.

Things got more complicated when I reached adulthood and entered the working world, where I discovered that there are some contexts that have little or no value for me, at least after weighing it against the psychological costs. For example, in one incarnation of my professional life I was a website project manager—it was a time of big personalities, naked aggression, covert agendas, loud voices, and even louder voices.

In retrospect, my choice to pursue that career seems nearly insane, but you can't underestimate how pressured I felt to leave my comfort zone and conform to the extrovert ideal throughout high school and college. I heard it explicitly from teachers and peers—"Assert yourself!" "You have to work the room!" "It's *wrong* to choose a career that enables your antisocial tendencies!"—and I also absorbed it through all the usual messaging vehicles that bombard us every day via radio, television, advertising, movies, and yes, even books.

So, with many misgivings, I turned my back on my natural inclinations and pursued a career that lumped me in with a highly contentious group of colleagues. My workdays felt like a continuous battle to claim every molecule of air in the room, which is so far outside of my comfort zone that it might as well be in another solar system.

The kind of productivity that I'm able to cough up in such a cacophonous, confrontational work setting is ... let's call it suboptimal. It was through a stroke of extreme good fortune that I gained a toehold in the world of librarianship, where I found colleagues who actually place value on contemplative work processes and weigh ideas based on their merit, not on the volume they're proclaimed with.

Now, there are certainly some complexities in my case. It's not too hard to find examples in which my decision to refrain from speaking up was not in my best interests but was instead rooted in apprehension or disengagement. For example, during one holiday break from college my uncle was diagnosed with lung cancer, which had metastasized in a bad way; when I learned about it he had very little time left. My mother and one or two of my aunts made hurried plans to visit him in the hospital, but they discouraged me from going.

I believe their intentions were good, if misguided—there was clearly a collective desire to spare me emotional distress. I was in the midst of a long, difficult stretch of my life, one in which a word of discouragement on any topic at all was enough to make me dismiss my own feelings on the matter. So I mutely accepted their discouragement, and in the state of psychological detachment that was normal for me at the time, retired to my room to contemplate things.

Thank goodness for my cousin Cathy (there she is again!), who came to me and asked if I really wanted to see my uncle. I shrugged and said, "I don't know," which Cathy wisely interpreted as "yes." She told me that if I really wanted to say good-bye, which I realized I did, I should insist upon it.

She was right. There are times of great importance, whether in service of personal beliefs, emotional satisfaction, professional opportunity, or plain old human decency, when it is possible to speak too softly.

However, I still believe there are too few contexts in which a measured tone, quiet contemplation, and solitary diligence are openly and publicly celebrated. I've had to hunt for them—a process complicated by other difficulties I've had in navigating through life—but in the end, I found one that's exactly right for me. In fact, I found my life's work. The core activity of my career as an author is sitting alone, in a state of fierce concentration, mining my internal world for the creation of fiction.

Paradoxically, I now find myself in a place where my ability to speak up and be heard is greater than it's ever been—I think that's partly because the Internet is one of the greatest things that has ever happened to introverts, because it plays to our strengths. We can share our thoughts, feelings, and ideas in full, taking as much time as we need to craft them! We can communicate on a broad level without feeling assaulted by sensory input! We can talk to the entire planet in our food-stained pajamas!

The Internet's high-tech niftiness isn't at the root of this new-found ability, however—it's just been a tool for developing that ability. It's a terrific tool that provides completely new opportunities I've never had before, true, but in the end, it's still just a tool. After years of soul-searching, self-doubt, and painful uncertainty, I've finally found a measure of self-acceptance, and a steadily increasing belief in the value of my unique presence in the world.

Maybe what I'm proposing is not that we break the rule to speak up, but that we amend it. We don't all need to suck the air out of every room we walk into or treat conversation as a gladiatorial sport. We have methods of making our presence felt that are quieter and more contemplative, but no less powerful. In other words, there's more than one way to speak up.

ALWAYS SIT IN YOUR ASSIGNED SEAT …

LYN MILLER-LACHMANN

In my elementary school, the teachers assigned seats not only in the classroom but also in the cafeteria. Doing so made it easier for them to keep track of us, to figure out, say, who went missing or who sent food flying in someone else's direction.

When I started middle school, I was overjoyed at first that we would be able to choose our own seats rather than having to sit where the teacher told us. I saw it as a privilege of growing up, getting to making our own decisions for at least one period in the school day. My joy disappeared by the end of the first week, however, when I discovered that my fellow students were far more determined to sort us out and make sure we didn't sit where we weren't supposed to sit. Their "assigned seats" generally excluded me, due to my unusual and obsessive interests and lack of social skills that I would later find out are signs of the autism spectrum condition known as Asperger's syndrome. (I always knew I was "different" but was not officially diagnosed until adulthood.)

Sometime in seventh grade, I got tired of sitting by myself. I wanted to be popular, so I decided to sit at the popular girls' table. In my supreme cluelessness, I believed that sitting at the same table would make me one of them. I paid for my food, brought my lunch tray to the table claimed by the popular girls, and set it down. Without saying a word, one of the girls pushed my tray from the table onto the floor.

This breaking of the unwritten rule, "Always sit in your assigned seat," inspired—and begins—my middle grade novel *Rogue*, about a 13-year-old girl with Asperger's who will do anything to have a friend. Unlike my protagonist, I did not pick my tray off the floor and slam it into the girl's face (thereby getting kicked out of school for the rest of the year). Instead, I returned to my solitary spot at the other end of the cafeteria for the remainder of my middle school years, and in high school I found other places to eat lunch where I didn't have to see anyone else and they didn't see me. One of the girls from the popular table graduated with me, and we ended up going to the same university, but our paths never crossed in the four years we were there. Until I spotted her name in the alumni magazine, I completely forgot that she and I were in the same class in college as well as in middle and high school. She had become just as invisible to me as I was to her in high school.

In the 1990s the psychologist Beverly Daniel Tatum published a bestselling book titled *Why Are All the Black Kids Sitting Together in the Cafeteria?* In it, she wrote, "most of the early information we receive about 'others'—people racially, religiously, or socioeconomically different from ourselves—does not come as the result of firsthand experience. The secondhand information we do receive has often been distorted, shaped by cultural stereotypes, and left incomplete." In other words, when we sit at tables with people just like us and don't get to know anyone who is different or who might make us feel uncomfortable, the prejudices we already have get set in stone. People who are different from us don't become part of our lives. They are as invisible as I was to the popular girl, and eventually as invisible as she was to me. And when we don't see people, we often don't care when they get treated unfairly. Or we may become the ones who treat others unfairly because they are "not like us."

Look around the cafeteria at your school. Are all the black or brown kids sitting together? How about the ones known or suspected to be gay? Are all the athletes at certain tables? Do the popular kids have their own table? Where do the kids with special needs sit?

Even though I broke a rule by sitting at the popular girls' table and was humiliated in front of the entire middle school as a result, it didn't stop me from sitting at other tables to which I had not been assigned. I began to experience benefits from doing this, and I found out that one good thing often leads to another. After I got my master's degree in American studies, I took a job at a troubled high school in New York City. In fact, I went for my first interview the day after a student had killed a teacher at a neighboring school. As a white teacher at a school with a mostly Puerto Rican and African American student body, I had to overcome my students' distrust of me, as well as my mother's fears for my safety. I believe I learned as much, if not more, from the students than they learned from me, and I will always appreciate their willingness to work with me and the good times we had together.

I became friends with the Puerto Rican teacher who shared a classroom with me. He introduced me to his favorite Latin American music, as well as the stores that sold it in New York. When I moved to Wisconsin two years later, I joined an organization that put on concerts, and I met a lot of internationally famous musicians. I picked up musicians from the airport, and some of them stayed at my house. I took Spanish classes and traveled to Latin America. Today I'm the assistant host of a bilingual radio program of Latin American and Spanish music, poetry, and history on WRPI-FM, and I also DJ Latin dance parties. The stories that I heard from the musicians and the people I worked with to organize concerts—most of them people who had fled brutal dictatorships in Latin America in the 1970s and 1980s—inspired my award-winning young adult novel *Gringolandia*. I would have had none of these valuable experiences—and *Gringolandia* would have remained unwritten—if I'd stuck to sitting with people just like me and I hadn't learned to speak Spanish, even though it was hard and some people made fun of my accent.

Not sitting in your assigned seat in the cafeteria means stepping away from the plans and expectations of people with whom you have everything in common—family, friends, neighbors—and getting to know people whose lives and experiences are different from yours. It also means doing things that people might not expect you to do. When I became the assistant host of "Los Vientos del Pueblo" on WRPI, I met the hosts of the show that preceded mine, "HomoRadio." Through them, I became involved in the campaign to legalize same-sex marriage in New York State and I had the thrill of watching a live stream of the vote in the state senate as the dreams of so many gay and lesbian couples came true in the summer of 2011. Now I'm very busy as a DJ for wedding receptions of both opposite-sex and same-sex couples.

As a writer, I've found that having characters do surprising or unexpected things adds interest and depth to a novel. For instance, my main character with Asperger's doesn't just sit around alone, even though she has trouble making friends. She likes to ride her bike and she's handy with a camcorder. As a result, she finds common ground with a group of boys who do BMX stunts and extreme mountain biking, and she records them in action. She may have special challenges, but she also has things in common with the boys, and her different abilities allow her to help them while they help her to make friends and develop confidence in social situations.

Although this example is from a work of fiction, it is based on my own long history of not sitting at my assigned table and not doing the things that people expected me to do. In some ways, having Asperger's makes it easier for me to cross social and cultural boundaries. I have to study social interactions that others take for granted; for me, every culture is a foreign culture. My experience of being invisible or actively excluded gives me a connection to others who have faced invisibility and exclusion because of race, ethnicity, language, religion, class, sexual orientation, or disability. I know what it is like to have to hide who I am and try to fit into what the majority defines as "normal"—and what it is like to fail miserably at doing so. For many years in middle and high school, I sat at my table alone and wished someone would cross a boundary to join me.

There were three boys in my elementary school class who, when assigned by the teacher to sit at the table with me, included me in their conversations. They told me about their friends and their sports teams, and one of them regularly invited me to his house to play football with him and his friends. (I did. It was one of the sports where I actually excelled.) When I developed a speech impediment in fourth grade, the three boys spoke up for me. Through them, I learned the secrets of making friends and what it was like to have them. I developed skills and confidence in dealing with other people, and I imagine that these boys continued, as teenagers and adults, to cross boundaries, embrace differences, and make the world a more welcoming place. We all scattered after fifth grade and lost touch, but decades later I still remember their names and their kindness toward me.

Ten years ago, shortly after the publication of *Why Are All the Black Kids Sitting Together in the Cafeteria?*, a group of teachers and writers associated with the magazine *Teaching Tolerance* started Mix It Up at Lunch Day. For one day in October, college students and students in middle and high school are encouraged to sit at a different table and to meet someone they didn't know before. As the organizers wrote on the *Teaching Tolerance* website, www.tolerance.org, "We ask students to move out of their comfort zones and connect with someone new over lunch."

One day doesn't seem like a lot of time to connect with someone new. However, there's a lot that you can learn about another person's culture and experiences from a single lunch period. And as the three boys from my elementary school proved, you can make a big difference in someone else's life by reaching out. One day can become the start of much bigger things if you make new friends and discover new interests, if learning about the challenges and injustices that other people face leads you to right some wrongs, or if you make it possible for your new friend to overcome personal obstacles to reaching his or her potential.

So *don't* always sit in your assigned seat! Break this rule! Any day can be Mix It Up at Lunch Day. That single day could change your life for the better—and someone else's life too.

BE NORMAL

JENNIFER A. NIELSEN

Let's get one fact out of the way first: I admit it. I was a weird kid. Not weird in the sense that I huddled in corners, or sang songs to myself at the lunch tables, or carried around a collection of spiders in a jar (no chance of me ever doing the latter, *that* is certain).

It was more that I didn't quite fit in with everyone else. I was too much of a tomboy to care about anything the girls were doing, and too much of a girl for the boys to want me playing with them. And the things that interested me were just, well, weird.

I liked to conduct science experiments on the mud at first base after a rainstorm (Hypothesis: Is this oil?). I often explored the far corners of the playground (Where does the hole in this fence lead to?). And I seemed to have trouble keeping the knees of my pants clean.

Worst of all, I had stories in my head all the time. Fantastical adventures in which I was always the star. Some took me into other made-up worlds, some placed me in extreme danger, and some turned me into a princess in a faraway kingdom.

Usually, the stories were far more interesting than the real world. So I spent a lot of time in my head, building and shaping my ideas, refining them into detailed plots with suspenseful moments that I could secretly live out during each 15-minute afternoon recess.

While other kids climbed monkey bars, I turned them into imaginary cliffs and scaled them with all the thrill and danger as if I were on a ledge at Mount Everest. My classmates only played on the swings. I went as high as I could with the intention of jumping off, like a desperate passenger on an airplane in free fall.

Often, I just sat on the hillside of the playground, staring at nothing, and living out the adventure in my mind. Occasionally I was pulled away by the pleas of friends to play. But usually they didn't ask, and generally speaking, I rarely noticed.

It wasn't such a big deal to be different when I was in elementary school. Most kids have their quirks in those years—some are just better at hiding them than others.

When it really started to matter was in middle school, that time of life when the worst thing that could possibly happen is to somehow be seen as different. The all-encompassing rule of teenage life is that fitting in requires you to build a group of your peers, and then be exactly like they are.

So I tried to be "normal." I really did.

I stopped exploring on my hands and knees, stopped staring into thin air as if my mind was in another world, and instead started walking, talking, dressing, eating, laughing, and living like everyone else.

It wasn't easy. My family didn't have a lot of money, definitely not enough for all the latest fashions. I might have had a few trendy items, but I could only wear them so many times in a week.

I tried to care about what all the girls in my neighborhood cared about, but I really didn't. Then I told myself that pretending to be like them would make me like them. And for a while, I thought I was succeeding.

Until that summer, when I went on a camping trip with all the teen girls in my church. I had thought everything was going well until the final night when awards were handed out by the oldest girls, as tradition dictated.

All the usual awards went out, for the cutest, funniest, or most adventurous girl, the late-night hoot, and the early-morning chirper.

Then came my award: weirdest girl.

In whatever way the award was meant, it broke my heart. As hard as I had tried to run from that childhood reputation, I understood in that moment that this was the way my peers saw me and probably always would see me. Whether they intended it as a gentle tease or an outright insult didn't matter. It hurt. And from that point on, I wanted nothing more to do with any of those girls.

It wasn't long after that when the natural process of growing up began working on me, and I matured and found my own voice. The energy I had put into stories in my head transferred into my performances in theater. But although it was a far more socially acceptable oddity, I still saw myself as being somewhat separate from most other kids. I had great friends and fit in just fine. But in my head I was still—well, you know—weird.

And anything but normal.

Years have passed, and I look back on that time with a completely new understanding. I'm an author now, and the best part of my job is creating hypothetical scenarios for all sorts of ideas. I might not explore paths through holes in fences (trust me, that wouldn't be a good idea), but I explore plots and characters and time periods. As for keeping the knees of my pants clean—I'm still not much interested in that.

And I will always enjoy sitting on the side of a hill putting stories together, stories that I can write down and weave into the pages of a book. Books that the children of those girls at camp may one day pick up and read.

I had tried so hard as a teenager to follow all the rules of growing up. I had thought it was better to be normal, because the opposite really didn't sound all that appealing. I had thought it was better to be normal because even if it was boring, at least I wasn't weird.

But anyone can be normal, can blend in, can color within the lines. Anyone can stand in the middle of a crowd and say, "Don't look this way. There's nothing special about me."

What I didn't understand in my teen years is that the things that I did that were "weird" were helping me to think in unconventional ways, stretching my imagination, and preparing me for a career one day, one in which I very much want to stand out.

Although the girls at camp hurt me at the time, I have them to thank now. Because without their label, I probably would have continued trying to be just like them. Normal.

What the world needs is more people who are willing to stand out, to break the rules that would make everyone look, think, and act like everyone else. And frankly, we need more people who are willing to be just a little bit weird.

DON'T CLASH WITH THE CROWD

ANNA STANISZEWSKI

It was seventh grade Clash Day, and I looked awesome. Paisley leggings, mismatched socks, a plaid shirt layered over a striped T-shirt, and of course, a rainbow assortment of scrunchies. I couldn't wait for everyone to see me. They would be totally blown away.

Then I got to school. And I froze. All the other kids were walking through the halls dressed normally, all in the most nonclashing outfits imaginable. And all of them—*all of them*—were staring at me like I'd just stumbled out of a carnival act.

"What are you wearing?" one of my friends whispered, her eyes round as buttons. I could tell she was on the verge of running off and pretending she didn't know me.

"It's Clash Day," I said weakly. Apparently, no one else had cared enough to dress up. Or even to remember.

Then I spotted another girl at her locker: Polka dot pants! Striped shirt!

"Oh thank goodness," she said, rushing over to me. "Someone else clashed. I can't believe how ridiculous I look!"

I gawked at her. If *she* looked ridiculous in her two contrasting patterns, then I was the raw, molten form of humiliation. Don't get too close or you might catch fire.

There had to be other people who'd remembered Clash Day, I told myself. But as I walked through the seventh grade hallway, I realized there weren't. I was the lone eyesore in a sea of color-coded perfection.

Hopefully, no one would send me down to the guidance office for a psych evaluation.

"Did you dress like that on purpose?" a snide girl in my home-room asked. I didn't know what that said about my fashion sense if she thought I could reach into my closet with my eyes closed and pull on a crazy outfit just because it was Monday.

"Yes," I told her, almost in a whisper. I felt something inside me breaking. I wanted to run off to the bathroom and cry like a baby. But I couldn't be that girl. I wouldn't be.

For years, I'd tried to fit in. Even though I had a long last name no one could pronounce. Even though I had parents who talked with funny accents and made me eat liverwurst-and-tomato sand-wiches for breakfast. And even though I wasn't allowed to have bangs or get my ears pierced or do pretty much anything else that was socially acceptable. After all that time of trying to blend with the crowd, there was nowhere for me to hide. It wasn't even a gym day, so I couldn't retreat into the safety of bland workout clothes.

After lunch, I sat in class with my head down, just trying to make it through to the end of the day. Then I realized something. People weren't staring anymore. They weren't paying attention to me at all. The clash shock had worn off, and now I was just plain old Anna again.

And that's when a foreign, somewhat crazy thought crept into my brain: Maybe nobody actually *cared* what I did. Even if it felt like all eyes were on me the minute I embarrassed myself, maybe that was mostly in my head. After all, other people had their own reputations to worry about, didn't they?

When the bell rang and I went on to my next class, I barely even blushed when people looked at me with confused eyes. Chances were, they would forget all about me in the span of a minute and go right back to their own lives. A hideous outfit wasn't really worth remembering when there were crushes and homework and bullies to navigate.

Finally, the day was over and I could rush home and change. Phew. The worst day of my life was officially over.

The next morning, I went to school all back to my normal self. It felt good, and yet it didn't. There was no reason for anyone to acknowledge my existence. I was back to blending, and it felt so *boring*.

If I'd been a character in a teen movie, I would have thrown on a horrible outfit again and orchestrated some sort of dramatic gesture in the middle of the cafeteria (complete with a group dance number). But I didn't want to stand out for my color-blind wardrobe. I just wanted people to see that there was something more to me than the painfully shy girl who only felt comfortable talking to her close friends.

Now, don't get your hopes up. The real me didn't magically emerge from a nerdy cocoon and blossom into a confident butterfly overnight. Or over the course of the year, or even the decade. But still, something felt just a tiny bit different that day.

So what if I didn't have bangs and my hair was long and hippie-ish? Who cared that my unpierced ears meant no one ever knew what to get me for a present? And hey, I didn't really like those liverwurst sandwiches anyway, but would it be so terrible if I did? (OK, yes it would. Liverwurst is seriously the worst thing ever.)

Ultimately, it came down to this: I didn't care about getting noticed, but I was tired of blending. There *were* things about me that deserved attention, that were maybe even a little bit memorable. OK, maybe not my keen fashion sense. But I could write. I could act. I could play the flute. And sometimes I could make people laugh. I wasn't totally invisible. And I didn't have to be. Not anymore.

COMPARE YOURSELF TO OTHERS

LUKE REYNOLDS

I'd just finished applying the perfect amount of gel to my hair, and my feisty cowlick had momentarily admitted defeat. In front of the mirror, I practiced my tough-guy guise, whereby I viewed the mirror like I was (possibly) going to crush it with my bare hands if it said the wrong thing. Luckily, my mirror remained silent, and I gave the me in the mirror a nod before I grabbed my backpack, held my fierce look, and left the bedroom on whose walls were plastered posters of Whitney Houston and Martin Luther King Jr.

I had hair whose strands had been frozen in exactly the right place. I was cool. I was tough. I was ready for the eighth grade.

In the hallways of our home, I was immediately assaulted by my younger brothers—two and four years old—"Wukie! Wukie!" and "Luke, let's play with blocks!" I managed to resist their sly attacks on my toughness and maintained my sense of cool. I was, after all, ready for eighth grade. And this year, I was *finally* going to be the guy that guys were supposed to finally be. No more smile-all-the-time, cowlicky-hair, too-nice-to-go-out-with-Luke. No. Those days were over.

It took only a few days of eighth grade to realize that, well, who was I kidding? The more I watched the other guys in my middle school, the more I became convinced that no matter how hard I tried, I would never be like them. There was no way I was going to give up being goofy with my little brothers, listening to speeches by Martin Luther King Jr. and Malcolm X on my Sony Walkman while I ran my paper route, or ever, ever, *ever* get my stupid cowlick to lay down flat (even if I applied enough gel to sink the *Titanic* a few times over). And, to be honest, the more my older brother Michael blasted Whitney Houston's "I Will Always Love You" through our shared bedroom, the more I came to love the song, too.

So my eighth grade year became a year of trying to decide which way I was going to go: continue the constant comparisons of myself to the other guys in my school, or just be what came naturally to me. As I was trying out the tough-guy guise at school, yet flipping back to the speech-listening, silly guy at home, my oldest brother Christopher provided some much-needed wisdom and advice.

As a deaf man, Chris has endured a number of tough obstacles from public school culture, and when he first brought me running with him during my eighth grade year, he began to share his own journey with me. My jaw dropped so many times during our runs together, as he told me about the ways in which he'd broken out of the comparison game. His deafness had already forced him into a box whereby he was immediately seen as "different" from most everyone else in his high school. And yet Chris still tried to become as similar as possible to everyone around him. For a while, he hid himself in order to try and claim the artifice of the mob—much like I had been desperately trying to do during my own eighth grade year.

On one particular run—in which I had, *literally*, the runs—Chris was especially challenging and helped me to keep on going even though I thought my stomach was going to fall out of my anus and my legs were going to detach and form their own community in which my brain would not be invited to reside. Chris just wouldn't let me quit. He believed in me; he encouraged me; he told me there'd be Cool Ranch Doritos if I finished the run.

And thanks to Chris, I did. I finished that run and many more afterward. Over the course of a lifetime—starting way back during that eighth grade year—Chris has continued to teach me the power of pushing past the barriers that seem impossible to break. And the comparison game, for me, has been the biggest barrier.

As grown men (at least in body, possibly not in social maturity), Chris and I ran the London Marathon together in 2001. We had vowed to each other before the race that, no matter what, we would finish. However intense the pain became, we would push one another and finish the 26.2 miles of painful fun. When race day arrived, we ran the first 10 miles in glee: waving to the crowds who had gathered to watch all the runners who were twice as fast as we were, yet hung around the see us tortoises compete. The atmosphere was electric: bands jamming, hands and flags flapping, food everywhere, the sky a clear, unusual blue.

But by mile 17, Chris and I were both dying. One of us would fall to the ground, then look up in agony, uttering, "Save yourself! It's too late for me! Tell everyone I loved them ... go on ... leave me." But somehow or other, we'd get back up (usually with the enticement of Cool Ranch Doritos) and continue onward.

Then we reached mile 23.

Mile 23 is the kind of friend who convinces you he or she loves you but then tells you he or she absolutely despises you one day. *Bam.* Just like that. See, mile 23 met Chris and me and said, in very clear language, *You're going down.* And to prove its point, mile 23 gave us a man carrying a *full-size canoe* who ran right past us.

At this exact moment, the comparison game bit us both. It yelled in full force, *Ha! You think you guys are doing something worthwhile or hard? You're doing nothing. Look at the guy who is running an entire marathon while carrying a full-size canoe!* (It was odd, now that I think of it, how closely the voice of the comparison game resembled my own voice.)

Chris held out his hand to me, sweaty and shaking, and I reached out and grabbed it. We ran the rest of the marathon like that. Two grown men holding hands. Two brothers hell-bent on finishing something they'd said they would finish.

And we did. After 5 hours and 49 minutes and 24 seconds, we did.

Crossing the finish line, we collapsed. Our sweat drained onto the grass, where we rolled around in pain and promised one another effusively—between cries that we were, in fact, dying—that we would never, under any circumstances, run a marathon again.

The winner of the 2001 London Marathon wasn't the guy who was carrying the canoe (thank God). However, the winner ran the race in 2 hours, 7 minutes, and 11 seconds. That means, roughly, that he could have run three marathons in the time it took me and Chris to finish just one.

Three.

If I was a believer in the comparison game, I might begin to think Chris and I had failed—that we could have, should have, would have done better. But then I would have missed the whole point of what that marathon was all about (and what this marathon we call life is all about, too). Because ultimately, what matters isn't the time in which we ran the race but the quality of the relationship we shared as we ran it.

This is where the comparison game begins to lose its ammunition. When you go to school, and you compare yourself to every other student in your grade, you lose track of the people who love you and who want to run alongside you. The more you watch the runners who are faster than you—the students whose biceps, breasts, or brains are bigger than yours—the more you lose track of the joy of the race you're *in right now.*

My brother-in-law, Paul, once shared a beautiful quote with me: "Comparison is the thief of joy." And it's true. As we gaze at others and compare ourselves to them, we allow the joy to be stolen right out of our own lives. We go to bed with the front door open, inviting thieves into our home saying, *Steal everything! I'm too busy taking notes on how everyone else is living to protect my own life!*

And there's a lot to protect. You have relationships with people who care deeply about you. They may not be the most popular people; they may not be the people who look exactly like the (fake) people on magazine covers—but they love you. There are people who are willing to run the whole dang 26.2 miles of life alongside you. And *these* are the people you want to hang out with and trust. But the trick is that you only notice them when you stop comparing yourself to others.

I don't know what happened to the guy who won the 2001 London Marathon with a time of 2 hours, 7 minutes, and 11 seconds. And I don't know what happened to the guy who passed my brother and I while he was carrying a canoe. (Come on, though, *seriously?*) But I do know that my brother Chris and I still have a great relationship, and when life gets hard, we can connect and pull one another up off the ground. We can smile and invoke the sacred possibility of Cool Ranch Doritos. And we can remind one another that the race worth running is the one in which you grab a hand of the person beside you and keep moving forward, refusing to believe the voice of the comparison game telling you to quit.

Because what really matters in life is never the time in which you run the race, but the quality of the relationships you nurture along the route.

BE PRODUCTIVE

JENNIFER ZIEGLER

"**D**o your homework!"
"Take out the trash!"
"Practice the euphonium!"
"Wash behind your ears!"

You hear it all day long—the litany of directives from parents, teachers, and other responsible grown-ups. Did they spot you flopped across the couch? Because nothing elicits orders like the sight of a young person lazing about. It is a truth universally acknowledged that a kid in possession of free time must be in need of a task.

Well, I'm a responsible grown-up (if you put quote marks around "grown-up" and define responsible as meaning "neither the police nor the IRS is hunting me down"), and I say that's a load of poo.

Don't get me wrong. I know that every day there are things we must accomplish. If we don't we suffer the consequences of bad grades, reprimands, late fees, disgusting ear backsides, and so on. However, I quibble with the notion that we must *always* be occupied.

I am going to give you a piece of advice now that will blow your mind. Try to stay conscious while processing the words, and then force yourself to continue reading. I'll make sense of it—I promise. Ready? OK. Here's my advice: be bored.

Still with me? I know suggesting that you become bored on purpose is like asking you to eat nothing but lima beans for the rest of your life. But I'm totally serious. You should, on a regular basis, become utterly bored.

Because guess what? When you do, something amazing will happen: you won't stay bored. Your mind won't allow it. Your imagination will spin up thoughts and ideas you've never had before—exciting ones that can lead to all sorts of experiments, adventures, and means of expression. However, if all we do each day is hop from task to task with no downtime, these notions will never untangle themselves from the jumbled center of our mind.

Again, don't misunderstand. I'm not advocating putting down the textbooks in favor of the game controller—or even a good book. I'm promoting the notion of doing nothing.

Absolutely nothing.

For the first half of my childhood, my family and I lived in Anchorage, Alaska. As you probably know, this is not that far from where polar bears roam. It's cold. I mean near-arctic, subzero, icicles-on-the-tip-of-your-nose cold. And in the wintertime, it is mainly dark. We romped about outdoors as much as we could, but sometimes conditions were just too hazardous. Plus, back then we didn't have a home computer or the Internet or a gaming system or even a tricked-out TV with a cable package and widgets. We did have a TV that picked up three stations (four if you struck a flamingo-like pose just off to the right), but my mom severely limited the amount of time we could watch it. So what did we do all day when we were trapped inside with no cool gadgets?

Well, we were bored. But never for long. We devoured books and after we finished them we continued the stories—either in our heads or in a live-action portrayal with slapdash costumes and buildings made of TV trays and blankets. We invented games and cooked up concoctions in the kitchen. Once, I spent weeks on an elaborate miniature house made out of shoeboxes.

But it was making up stories that suited me best during those vast stretches of downtime. At night, when we were supposed to be asleep, I would entertain my sister Amanda with all kinds of wacky tales. I told her that Jerry, the neighbor's cat, was really a spy. And I made up the character Reginald, a six-month-old baby who became the leader of a rock band. Later (probably when there was no one around to listen to me) I started writing down my stories. I'd fill up spiral-bound notebooks with tales of romance and adventure (most of them abandoned halfway though), poems, cartoons, clothing designs, song lyrics, elaborate doodles, and persuasive essays on topics such as "Who is the Cutest Member of Duran Duran?" This activity continued throughout my high school years. Looking back, I see how this writing for the sheer joy of it, with the freedom to experiment with styles and topics, ended up shaping my author voice. Of course, back then I didn't realize this. I was simply filling up time by filling up pages with any idea that entered my mind.

Amanda's favorite pastime was playing school. She would become the strict "Mrs. Bottom," and our little brother Jason was her only pupil, "Johnny Record." I was rarely a part of these games, but I do remember the giggles emanating from the back room and the worksheets left behind on the tables with math problems like "If Johnny burps 10 times an hour, how many burps will he make in one day?" Besides providing countless hours of fun, this diversion also had Jason reading by the age of two. Amanda, it seemed, was quite good at making learning fun. Even throughout her teen years she continued schooling Jason—only her lessons changed from calculating burps to making mini pizzas and how to talk Mom into allowing a later curfew. It's probably no coincidence that she is now a beloved middle school teacher.

When Jason was bored he devised ways of earning cash. He sold lemonade and greeting cards. He would raid our rooms and then hold a garage sale. In middle school, he even had a venture that was something like an extortion ring. Later, in high school, he convinced the local movie theater manager to hire him even though he was only 15. And when he needed extra cash, he sometimes hustled pool at a nearby club. The kid always had money. Quite appropriately, he is now a successful businessman.

None of us are born knowing ourselves or knowing what we really love in life. Too often we pursue goals that we've absorbed as our own through well-meaning advice from others. But how can we know if it's what *we* truly want?

The only way to make these discoveries is to pay attention to where our minds lead us during those empty, quiet hours. You can't find and follow your dreams if you never give yourself time to dream. While I thoroughly enjoyed my camps, competitions, piano and dance lessons—and I learned a lot from them—it was those boring days of nothing that led me to my life's true passion: writing novels. Stories always popped into my head when there was nothing else to occupy it.

I've heard similar accounts from other people. Musicians will recall how, whenever they were bored, they'd reach for their guitars and come up with songs. Artists envisioned pictures so vivid, they had to try to draw or paint them. And it was while idling beneath a tree that Isaac Newton supposedly got conked on the head by an apple, which led to his theory of gravity.

You've probably got a jam-packed schedule and a world of diversions built into your cell phone. In the Stone Age of my youth, it took effort to not be bored—but now, you have to make a deliberate effort to do nothing. And yet it's worth it. While SAT classes, sports tournaments, advance-placement coursework, and service clubs help you get into colleges and become a well-rounded human, don't forget to preserve some quality *nothing* time too. Yes, turning off the gadgets and scheduling some free time is hard—but harder still is discovering at age 30 that you are not who you thought you were. Get to know yourself and make sure that the path you are on is the path you truly want.

We are human beings, not human doings. Sometimes it is enough to just ... be. Yes, it's important to do laundry, budget, floss, weed the garden, learn the proper use of commas, and all those other grown-uppy things. But if you only measure your worth by how much you have accomplished, you will end up with an incomplete view of yourself. Don't overload your schedule so much that you lose touch with you.

So safeguard those wide-open moments. Wander and wonder. You'll be surprised at where your mind will lead you. And you'll find that you are often far more interesting than you realize.

ALWAYS KNOW WHERE YOU'RE GOING

BRIAN YANSKY

WARNING—EXAGGERATION AHEAD.

Does anyone really know where they're going all the time? The idea is more an ideal, something that old people think young people *should* know, than a reality. It's one that often drives young people into choices before they're ready to make them or into feeling inadequate for not having every step of their future plotted out. I get a little testy about that.

People who *always* know where they're going are not the kind of people I want to talk to at a party, travel with in a car, work next to at a job, listen to at a sporting event. They are know-it-alls who don't know it all (though they often know a few things really well) but who think they do because—hey—they've always known where they were going. Give me the people who've been lost and felt their way blindly in the dark. The people who are travelers in life and are on, and have been on, a journey. People who want to discover and see more. The people who don't always know where they're going but have been there and back, wherever *there* is, and know there is always much, much more. I want to know those people who admit they don't know nearly enough.

People who always know where they're going think they are very clear about where they've been. They can give you detailed accounts of their successes in those places. They often forget their failures or pretend they never occurred, because in order to think you've always known where you were going, you must think you've always been in control and each choice was another step in the right direction. The "always know where you're going" people's memories must be very good when it comes to remembering choices that led to success and very bad when it comes to choices that led to failure.

People who don't always know where they're going freely admit they've made many mistakes and suffered numerous failures. In fact they're likely to claim they've learned more from their mistakes than from their successes. They believe in learning. And another thing: they admit they've had help along their way. They've been lost many times and had to ask for directions from teachers, mentors, friends, family, and strangers.

People who always know where they're going like to be around people like themselves. They're the kind of people who say to each other, often in whispers, "See that person? Not our kind of people." They crave the familiar, the dependable, the predictable, and so they want to see what they've always seen and know what they've always known. They're big on clubs and organizations. They like to think they belong to an elite. They don't talk to just anybody.

People who don't always know where they're going have traveled widely and met people from all walks of life: the rich, the poor, the city dweller, the small-town inhabitant, the educated, the uneducated, the kind, and the cruel—to name just a few. They understand the great variation in the world and appreciate the differences. Their lives have become richer and less predictable and more complex because of it. They love being inclusive. They will talk to most anybody. They like words like *quirky*. They can laugh at black humor. They can understand a bittersweet memory. Their interest in people makes them more interesting.

People who know where they're going are confident that they are always right. You can ask them about anything and they will tell you how you should think and what you should do and how you should live. They will list the exclusive clubs they belong to in order to convince you they know what they're talking about. They tend to see the world in black and white. They may or may not have a clear moral center, but either way they will divide the world into the have and have-nots, the successes and failures, winners and losers.

People who don't always know where they're going are not confident that they're always right. They will fight for something they believe in, something dear to them, but they won't always have a quick answer about what to do or who is right or wrong in a debate. They mull things over. They see both sides and are sometimes confused by this perspective. The world is full of gray areas for them. Sometimes the struggle to see into those gray areas causes them problems and sleepless nights. But it's this struggle that I love about them. They will never be as certain as the people who always know where they're going, but in that uncertainty lies the possibility to be better, to do better, and to improve themselves and others. They learn from their mistakes because they admit they've made them.

The people who always know where they're going don't see the need for self-improvement in areas beyond their mapped path. They are often focused and driven and ambitious to get where they want to go. They will seek ways to better themselves to this end. Their improvement is limited, however, to practical applications. They're in a hurry. No time to stop and smell the roses for them. Of course, they'll stumble sometimes. Even someone who always knows where they're going won't have every plan worked out. But they'll get right back up and push on. They have this admirable focus, even if it means everything outside it is out of focus. They will be very clear about what they're very clear about. Their experiences will be narrow, but they will know them intimately. Right is right. Wrong is wrong. They are what they are.

People who don't always know where they're going see the need for self-improvement all the time. They know they are hopelessly imperfect but they keep trying anyway. They know they've wasted time. They're aware that more than once they've taken the long way home, the long way to a friend's, the long way on a trip. For them, though, the open road means that they need to be open to changes and sometimes these changes will mean changes in themselves. They admit their imperfections. But they want to be better. One of the forces that drives them is the desire to be better.

People who have always known where they're going might be very good at their work and might be very successful. They tend to be organizers and planners who think inside the box. No surprise. They don't want to think outside the box. They're most comfortable ordering the box very, very well. They have a plan and they stick to it and they want others to stick to it. The unpredictability of outside the box annoys them and, deep down, that unpredictability frightens them. Anything might happen out there.

People who don't always know where they're going know that sometimes the only way to find their way is to be lost. They can think outside of the box because they spend a lot of their life outside of the box. In fact, some of them spend most of their life there. They are the creative thinkers: the artists, writers, actors, musicians, yes, but also the innovators in business and technology. They have been off-road. They can forge their way through unknown lands. Yes, they will get lost. They're OK with that. In fact, they feel most alive when they aren't certain what's up ahead. It's fun and exciting and liberating and sometimes a little scary not to know what is around the next turn. Anything might happen and they love that. This is how they make discoveries. This is how they find out what they are and are not looking for.

*   *   *   *   *

I warned you about exaggeration. The world of Homo sapiens can't really be so neatly divided into two groups of people, of course. But my point is this: it's OK to be lost sometimes; it's OK to struggle to find your way. I know I did.

In my youth I left school to travel around the country. I hitchhiked because I didn't have much money and because I wanted to see a side of America I hadn't seen. I traveled everywhere. I met all kinds of people. I had experiences, some good and some bad, but all interesting. For me, my travels were as much an education as my formal college education. And as I've said elsewhere, it was a cheaper and more scenic one.

I tell you this just to point out one way of leaving the well-traveled road. Everyone will have different ways of doing it but what they will all have in common is that the less traveled road will take the person to places he or she couldn't have known were there. The act of taking the less traveled roads will help you find yourself, who you are, and who you want to be, and the experience will make you more understanding of the lives of others. Writers need that. People need that.

It's true that people who *always* knows where they're going (if there are such people) may get there faster. But where they want to go will be limited by their own need for speed and their narrow focus. They won't have those unexpected, surprising consequences of wandering and of sometimes being lost. They won't understand black humor or bittersweet memories, and they will just become irritated at the suggestion of mysteries. *What do you mean what is the sound of one hand clapping? Black holes? Don't talk to me about black holes.*

In Robert Frost's poem "The Road Not Taken," the narrator comes to a place where he has to make a choice between two roads. He says, "I took the one less traveled by / And that has made all the difference." Me too. Not that it has always been good. Not that

I've always made the right choices. No. But I'm an old guy now, and I'm still excited to get up every morning and do the things I do, and I'm still hopeful that I can do them better and be better. And that makes all the difference.

DON'T GET FAT

LISA BURSTEIN

I throw up the $20 worth of food I just purchased and wipe away the puke and toilet water that has splashed onto my chin. "Don't get fat," a voice inside me chants. It is a voice that insists, that needles like a fly buzzing around in my head that I can't squash.

By starving myself all day and eating only a bagel each night for dinner, I finally achieved this rule. I had the kind of frame I'd always wanted: wrists I could circle my thumb and pinky around, cheeks that curved in like teacups, a collarbone that could poke your eye out.

I was thin. Too thin, but I was also "not fat." I had finally succeeded.

I was complimented for my new look by family members, by friends, by boys. I knew starving myself was wrong, but I also knew in this weird, deep, black place—the place where the voice lived—that if I wanted to be pretty, special, noticed, I couldn't get fat.

That is why I am throwing up now. That is why the bathroom door is locked and the overhead fan is on. That is why I will throw up tomorrow and the next day and the next and the voice in my head will hold my hair back. It will tell me that if I stop I will be a failure. It will tell me if I get fat, I will be worthless.

It has become a daily ritual: stop on the way home from high school and buy food, come home to an empty house, eat and throw up before my mom gets home from work. Sometimes, I will even do this while she is home, with the water running in the bathroom so she can't hear me. I can't stop. I want to stop and I can't.

I am afraid of getting fat again.

I am afraid of being in an empty house with nothing to do.

I am afraid that what the voice says is true.

I am afraid.

No one knows I am doing this. Not my friends, not my sister, and certainly not my mother or father—or maybe they do know and they just can't say anything. Maybe they don't know what to say. My eating disorder is the emaciated elephant in the room.

Not that I would know how to respond even if anyone did say something. The only explanation I have is that "I don't want to get fat." Even I know in my warped, sick, eating-disordered mind that my logic is flawed. Even I know the voice is the mayor of crazy-town.

Yet I listen.

Though I heard it many times over the years, I think that it was my mother who first taught me this rule. Because she knew I had the body type and appetite to get fat and because she knew that being fat would make life hard for me as a girl. She also followed this rule. Filling our cupboards and freezer with diet foods, puffing her cheeks out like a chipmunk when I ate more than she thought I should, yelling at my father when he went for second helpings. I don't blame her for this. She was taught this rule too.

There is no way she could have known I would have taken this rule and twisted it in the way I had. That is what is so scary about this rule, that it has the capacity to go too far so quickly.

And yet we are all taught this rule. As girls, especially teenage girls, we are taught on TV, in magazines, and in movies that the only girls who exist are thin girls. To be pretty is to be thin, to be noticed is to be pretty, to be noticed is the only thing that matters.

I've always been what you might call a greedy eater. I should have known that eventually my body would crumble and not be able to take the starvation anymore. So if I was cold, if my chest hurt, if my hair started to break, if I couldn't sleep, if I got winded when I walked, or if my stomach felt like I was constantly going down the big first hill of a roller coaster, I started eating. A lot. Too much. Then, I started throwing up.

*　*　*　*　*

I may have changed, but the voice never did. It still hammered me with this rule. It still made me figure out a way to follow it, at whatever cost.

I know this is a common story: girl starts a diet, goes too far, and slides into anorexia. Can't take the pain of anorexia and cuddles up to bulimia. But maybe that is why I am telling it. Because it is common. Too common. Because at its extreme, following this rule is where eating disorders start.

The problem with an eating disorder is that outwardly it is a disease of silence. A disease of secrets. It took me years to admit to anyone what I was doing. Even to admit it to myself. It is shameful to realize that you are willing to try to kill yourself to be thin. It is heartbreaking to absorb that you care so little about yourself, that you put yourself in this skewed lens when you think of your self-worth.

Even after you come to those realizations, it is even harder to tell someone else. To get better, you have to tell someone else. Telling someone else is how you start to break this rule. It is how I did.

I was lucky that the man who is now my husband cared enough to finally ask. He saw me struggling, chose not to ignore the signs, and asked me straight out if I was really doing this to myself. I don't know that I would have had the strength to tell him on my own, but because he cared enough to ask, he gave me the strength to finally tell the truth—to finally start to leave this rule behind.

Breaking this rule, no longer hearing it every time I looked in the mirror, was the only way I could start healing. I had to realize, too, that my body and how I felt about it was not my real problem. How I felt about myself, the person I was, the person I was afraid to let others see, was the problem. When the voice was talking to me, I didn't have to think about any of this.

I hate to admit it took me years of therapy and years beyond therapy to get there. That sometimes I still have trouble. I hate to admit that I have relapsed, several times. I hate to admit that the only way I am surviving now is that I have thrown out my scale and I have resolved that I will not let numbers rule my life. That I will not let the body I walk around in dictate how I feel about the person I am inside.

But I didn't learn those lessons as a teen. I didn't learn them as a college student. I didn't even learn them until two years ago.

At 34, I finally got it together enough to realize that destroying my body would never make me happy. Whatever happiness I thought succumbing to my "Don't get fat" mantra brought me was an illusion. As much an illusion as the food that disappeared when I flushed the shame of it away. As much an illusion as the voice I thought I heard.

It scares me that it took me so long to get here, but it scares me more to realize that I may never have. Following this rule consumed everything I had, took away all my feelings, made it so that even if I had survived physically, mentally I was dead. This rule was one that I had to allow to teeter a few times before I was able to ultimately tip it over. I am lucky that my body survived each game of chicken that I played with it.

It wasn't a magic wand that did it; it was simply deciding that I wanted to do more with my life than be thin. The rule had consumed me so much that if I kept following it, it was all I would ever be.

Since I've left this rule behind, I've become a wife and a published author, as well as an advocate for teen girls with self-esteem issues.

There are many who do not survive when adhering to this rule, and this essay is for them. For the ones who don't only die mentally but succumb to the slow suicide that is an eating disorder. It is also for that 14-year-old girl, standing on her scale and not liking the number she sees, looking at the tag on her jeans and not liking the size she sees, or grabbing at her stomach and wishing she could cut the fat away with a knife.

I do not want her to be alone in a bathroom, afraid for years like I was.

I do not want the voice to consume her.

I want to let her know that there is life beyond this rule. That she can reach out. That people understand.

That even though it took me years to get there, leaving this rule behind is when I finally found life.

TWO IS BETTER THAN ONE

NATALIE DIAS LORENZI

Try this: the next time you're browsing in a bookstore or waiting in line at the supermarket, grab a magazine, one for teens or for women. Chances are good you'll spot at least one cover that screams: How to Get Him to Notice You! or Is Your Boyfriend *The One*? Take Our Quiz and Find Out!

It's not only in magazines; the same message is everywhere, and the message is this: If you're not already part of a couple, then surely you must be out there looking.

In high school, I dated the same guy—let's call him Steve—from the beginning of my sophomore year until about 12 hours after my senior prom. Steve was a trumpet soloist in the marching band and had dimples when he smiled. Really, what more could a girl want? He was also a genuinely nice guy—the kind who wrote thank you notes to his grandmother and helped ducklings cross the street.

When he asked me to go to the homecoming dance, I said yes, and with that simple three-letter word, I entered the land of coupledom. I was no longer "just" Natalie; I was half of Steve and Natalie, Natalie and Steve.

"Ooh!" my friends squealed. "Steve is *so* nice! You're so lucky!" My guy friends didn't squeal, but they did declare Steve "a good guy."

All was well in the land of coupledom for two years, until Steve went off to college five hours away and I started my senior year. At first I missed Steve, and I wasn't quite sure what to do with myself. But soon, I started to realize that the missing wasn't so much about Steve; it was about Steve and Natalie, Natalie and Steve.

There were other guys I wanted to date, one crush in particular, but what would people say if I broke up with Steve? Everyone loved him, and everyone loved Steve and Natalie, Natalie and Steve. Anyway, what if my crush didn't like me back? I figured it was safer to stick with what I knew—a nice guy everyone loved, and me being one-half of a couple that everyone thought was perfect.

Besides, I didn't have to confront my doubts, not yet, anyway. Back in those pre–cell phone, pre-Internet days, Steve and I only talked once a week on the phone and wrote the occasional letter. It was easy to keep my feelings to myself, and Steve's heart intact. When he came home for holiday breaks, my friends basked in the glory of seeing Steve and Natalie, Natalie and Steve, together again.

"I don't know how you two can stand being apart," my friends would say.

Indeed.

When he went back to school after the holidays, I kept wishing he'd find someone else. That would make life so much easier—I'd be free to date other people, yet I wouldn't be the destroyer of perfect couples.

As my senior prom approached, however, I dreaded seeing Steve again. But I convinced myself that maybe this was just the way it was with long-distance relationships; once we saw each other again, I'd fall back in love. Or at least in serious like. I'd realize how stupid I was to even think of walking away from Mr. Nice Guy. But when Steve came to the door in his tux to pick me up, I knew. In his hand, he held a box with a ribbon, and inside was a heart-shaped necklace. Really, could he *be* any nicer? How could I break up with him now? I didn't deserve someone like him. I was an idiot.

So we went to dinner and on to the prom, and it was the worst night of my life. I was surrounded by happy prom-goers, dancing and laughing and making out on the dance floor, and all I wanted to do was to go home. Alone.

Steve knew something was wrong, but I wouldn't say what it was. I mean, who breaks up with her boyfriend at the prom? Or the day before his five-hour drive back to college to take his final exams? I was a coward—had been a coward for months. I would wait until he came home for the summer.

Except that I didn't.

The next morning, Steve stopped by my house before heading back to school. He knew *something* was wrong, and he wasn't leaving until I told him what it was. And so I told him. I told him that I still loved him as a friend, but I wasn't the right one for him. I'm pretty sure I used that old cliché, "You deserve better."

Steve did not take it well. Despite my gloomy mood at the prom, I don't think he saw this coming. Or maybe when he looked back after the fact, a part of him knew it had been brewing. But in that moment, I felt like I'd blindsided him. He insisted that everything would go back to normal if I only I took some time to think about it, not knowing that "thinking about it" was all I'd done over the last few months. I knew he must hate me, and I knew everyone at school would hate me for doing this to him. (Did I mention he was about to take his final exams?)

As I watched his car drive away, I felt sadness and regret and a lightness of heart that told me I'd done the right thing at exactly the wrong time. I should have let him go much, much sooner, for his sake as well as for mine. Now I had to face everyone the next day at school and brace myself for their reaction when they found out that Steve and Natalie, Natalie and Steve had dwindled to simply Natalie.

Word spread quickly, even without texts or tweets or Facebook status updates. And to my great surprise, no one hated me. Except maybe Steve's sister.

I went off to college two months later, free to date anyone I wanted. Except there was no one I really wanted to be with. I hated the whole small-talk dating scene, but I felt like I should be out there looking for the next guy. Because that's what we're supposed to do, right? I eventually did find the next guy, and a few more next guys after that. In the years between my 19th and 25th birthdays, I'd been single for only a few months.

During my last year of college, my friends started getting engaged and planning their weddings. I pored over bridal magazines with them and even stood beside them at altars in bridesmaids' dresses with shoes dyed to match. I wanted to get married, too, because that's what everyone seemed to be doing. Problem was, I wasn't convinced that my boyfriend at the time was the One. But I didn't think he *wasn't* the One—he still had potential. One evening after friends announced their engagement, we got into an argument over how a proposal of marriage should go. He said that it should be a total surprise, and I panicked. Was he thinking of proposing? I hoped not, because I wasn't sure what my answer would be. So I argued that the couple should first agree that marriage was definitely in their future. Then, and only then, could the guy propose.

To make a long story short, at 25 I broke up with this long-term boyfriend, but I was afraid. Maybe I should have stayed with him after all. Isn't that better than being alone? Would I ever meet anyone else? So I set about doing just that. I viewed every new guy I met through the same lens—could he be the One? If not, then I didn't even want to waste my time. If he could be the One, well then, I was interested.

And then one day I took a look at myself and didn't like what I saw—a young woman desperate to meet the right guy and worried all the time that she wouldn't. I needed to make a change, needed to get away from wedding planning and diamond rings and more bridesmaids' dresses with shoes dyed to match.

So I got a job teaching at an international school in Trieste, Italy, leaving my current job in an excellent school district that paid twice what I'd be earning in Italy. When I told one of my newly engaged friends about my shiny two-year contract, the first thing she said was, "Two years? When you get back, you'll be 28." The implication was that, at 28, I'd be *really* old and less likely to find someone to marry. That conversation sealed the deal for me—I knew I was making the right decision to leave.

My plan was to go on an Italian adventure for two years and then come back, reassess my life, and just sort of take it from there. I didn't have any plans for afterward, and that's just how I liked it. I felt free, like the day Steve drove away from my house and out of my life. Except this time, I didn't want to date anyone else; I wanted to spend some time remembering who I was.

There was one thing I knew for sure: I wouldn't meet the One in Italy. There are very few foreigners in Trieste, unlike Venice, which was a two-hour train ride away. And I couldn't exactly marry an Italian—I didn't speak the language and didn't want to live there for the rest of my life. So it was simple—I would go to Italy and simply enjoy *la bella vita*.

So what happened? I adored Italy and threw myself into learning the language and immersing myself in the culture. After a year, I started dating an Italian guy, not because I thought he was the One—how could he be? We both knew I only had a year left on my contract, and then I'd have to leave. So we made the best of the time we had. I went to his soccer games, he came to my school events, and we traveled and danced and shared countless plates of *pasta al pesto*.

When it was time to go, I wasn't ready to go home, and we weren't ready to say good-bye. I took a teaching job in Japan, and my boyfriend came to stay for two months. That's when I knew he was the One. And to think I'd stumbled across this relationship when I hadn't been looking. In fact, it wasn't until I'd *stopped* looking to be half of a couple that I found the person I wanted to spend the rest of my life with. To make an already long story short, he's now my husband of 16 years and we have three beautiful children.

If I could talk to my 15-year-old self, I would tell her to get to know and appreciate herself for the person she was, not the person she was with. If I had done that, I would have been able to tell when I stopped recognizing myself.

So don't worry about what the media and society say—that unless you're part of a couple already, surely you should be out looking for your other half. You are not one-half of a whole; you are already whole.

FOLLOW THE DIRECTIONS

TAMARA ELLIS SMITH

I have a friend Nate who, as a teenager, had a horrific home life. His parents gave him directions for living that he couldn't follow. Directions like exactly how to vacuum the floor, how to look at his mother and stepfather, how *not* to draw pictures because boys do *not* make art. He and his brother suffered terrible, traumatic abuse at the hands of the people they called family. Being inside the four walls of his house was not safe. Not ever.

A mountain stood behind his house. One day Nate's brother said, "C'mon. Let's go. I want to show you a place I found." They left their house and began to climb. The mountain was steep and tall and about halfway up spring water ran down the rocky trail, making it tough to climb. "Don't stop. You can do it," Nate's brother said. "Faster," he said. They slipped and skinned their knees as they scrambled to the top as fast as they could, but they didn't care. "We'll be safe up here," his brother said, tears and sweat running down his face. "They can't climb like we can."

When the two boys reached the top of the mountain they cried until there were no tears left, and they were left with a strange tingling feeling in their bodies. Then they sat silently and felt the wind blow their faces dry. They smelled the fern and trees and moss-laden air; the air of things growing free and strong, and they felt the tiniest seed of free and strong within themselves.

And then they looked out over the valley—out over their house and their abuse. They inhaled the mountain air and when they exhaled all of the tingling subsided. "That feeling," said Nate's brother, "is all the fear leaving. Here—with the trees and the wind—here is where we are safe."

Nate picked up a red maple leaf off of the dirt. He picked up another, and another, until he had a handful. Then he began to arrange them in a pattern according to their hue—the deepest blood red on one end and the palest sunrise red on the other.

* * * * *

I can't stop thinking about this story. Like the trees on Nate's mountain, this story's roots wind deep down through my body.

This story entwines with another—my own. And even though the narratives are different, they are also the same.

* * * * *

At a very young age I taught myself the art of walking through a minefield: eyes watching, watching, always watching for any slight change of movement or variation in the terrain, brain on high alert, ears tuned in for the activating sound that preceded an explosion.

I'm not talking about a war zone; I'm talking about junior high. All of my energy was devoted to anticipating external circumstances. As a result, I spent most of my middle grade and high school years feeling alienated from myself. I had no idea what I wanted, and no idea what I felt. When someone asked for my opinion I had a million smoke-and-mirror tricks that allowed me to avoid the question. I ignored. I feigned distraction. I changed the subject. I waited until someone else voiced her opinion and then I would agree. "That is *exactly* what I was going to say," I said over and over again.

Let's say two girls leaned against their lockers and pointed at someone. Their laughter swirled in the fluorescent light like a gas, and as it settled on the checkerboard floor I would look for the space that was left empty and fill it with my own nervous laughter. My body and brain were in a constant state of tension. What should I say? Who should I side with? How do I keep the peace? How do I fit in? Questions rapid-fired through my stomach 24-7, like a belly full of Xbox. That was on my inside. And on my outside? I was in a constant state of searching—eyes watching, feet tapping, ears straining—for the space that I was supposed to occupy.

I thought I needed other people to supply directions for who I had to be. I had no idea who I was.

But oh—there were a few times when I did, when I felt glimmers of that deep kind of knowing. That was when I hiked behind my house to the river in the woods. The change in air and temperature from indoors to outdoors was immediately calming. My heartbeat slowed to mirror the steady flow of the river as it moved west. The stirring of the wind in the leaves evened my breath. The sound of that ugly laughter rushed downstream and evaporated in the wind and in its place was a silence that signified a new kind of space. One that I could hope to someday fill with . . . me.

And in the meantime I began to bring a pen and notebook out with me on these hikes, and I filled pages and pages instead.

* * * * *

A cardboard box from IKEA shows up on your doorstep. You open it and there are pieces of plywood, screws, and the small tool IKEA always sends, the one that looks like a metal crank they promise that you absolutely cannot build without. There is a booklet of directions. You read all of them before you begin. Read them twice, isn't that the rule? Then you begin to assemble. Follow each step carefully. You end up with a new desk.

Life is full of directions that we are given to follow. Many of them are necessary. Useful. Ending up with a desk when you want to build a desk is a good thing. But directions aren't *always* good things. Often they are not only about how to do something but who to be. And they aren't always found on paper. Sometimes they are written by a parent with an angry yell or a menacing stare or, worse, a threatening hand. Sometimes they are written by a committee of girls and their laughter. The consequences of not following directions can sometimes be harsh, but following them can lead to equally harsh outcomes—they can take you outside of yourself and leave you feeling isolated, lonely, and disconnected.

Nate spent much of his teenage life rebelling against the directions laid out for him by his parents. I spent much of mine trying to decipher and comply with the directions I thought were laid out for me. We had very different childhoods, but they were so much the same too. Neither was a good way to live. Both were on other people's terms.

Nate and I both needed to find another way to live, in which the directions were ours and the tool necessary for building came from inside of each of us.

*   *   *   *   *

The theory of loose parts goes something like this: materials that can be moved, changed, combined, taken apart, and moved again foster the greatest creativity. Loose parts don't have a predetermined function, and they don't come with directions that must be learned and abided by. They are the anti-IKEA.

Being in places with many loose parts provides the opportunity to tap into this vital creative instinct. And when I imagine environments that have them in abundance, there is one place that always comes to mind: nature. The outdoors, in all of its wild details—its trees and rivers and rocks and wind—doesn't come with a stack of directions. And it doesn't come with that metal crank. It is at once far more complicated and far simpler than that. Animals like foxes put the loose parts of their landscapes together using their creativity and intuition and all the wisdom of evolution and of the animals that came before them, and they live—fully and wholly.

We are more like foxes—and trees and rivers for that matter—than we think. It's true. Little kids know this. It's why building forts is an almost universal pastime for them. Gathering sticks and stumps, rocks and dirt, and creating a home—a first home, with no directions, no precedents, like our ancestors did—is instinctive. (Or they make a fort out of a sheet and rope and that IKEA desk.)

When we get out of the cacophony of society—off of the street, off of the phone, out of the classroom, and out of the house—and get into nature, we feel it. Our bodies actually change. They quiet down and slow up. They literally mirror the landscape.

I was recently reminded that the air we breathe was once inside the leaf of a tree. We inhale as the trees exhale. Such a simple truth, such a simple exchange, and yet—it means everything. It means we are connected across time and species. Deep stuff.

I once spent a morning deciphering the footprints of a red fox along a trail, following it to the river where another fox joined it for a drink, and then back to the trail. I imagined the lives of those two foxes, and the other animals the river had witnessed, and I wrote a story about them both. Nate told me he used to spend hours arranging fallen autumn leaves into patterns of red, orange, and gold on the deep brown dirt at the top of his mountain, and later he carved the same shaped leaves out of wood that he inlaid into handmade furniture. By crossing into that scary, new, liberating place where our senses were wildly alive, both Nate and I were able to observe the beautiful loose parts in nature, and collaborate with them to create something new and unique.

And here is the utterly remarkable thing: we were then able to turn our attentions inward, to begin to recognize our *own* landscapes, to take in one beautiful loose part that was a piece of *each of us,* and hold it tight as we returned to our daily lives.

We all internalize the directions that are laid out in front of us. The ones our parents give us, the ones our teachers give us, the ones our peers give us. We internalize them, and they become a part of us. We don't even notice them. They are an endless, flat landscape inside our bodies. They just *are.* This—this incredible process of finding even one of your own loose parts—brings pieces of yourself into relief so that they pop up like little hills. This is the nature—no pun intended—of the truth, especially the truth about you. It sweeps in and stirs up the earth. It brings contrast and clarity. *Those are my stepfather's directions. They are more about him than about me. I don't believe in them. But I do believe in these leaves and patterns and art.* This is what began to happen for Nate. *Those girls live by those directions. I don't feel good when I try to live by them too. I do feel good when I follow a trail and imagine the stories that are lingering here and go home and write about them.* This is what began to happen for me.

Learning the art of do-not-follow-the-directions was my pathway and Nate's pathway to salvation—or perhaps, more aptly, *selfation.*

*　*　*　*　*

You are like those foxes. You are like the old maple trees. You are a fort builder. You have the same creativity, the same intuition, and the same wisdom—but it is easy to forget. I know I did. I misplaced my loose parts, and clutched those IKEA-like directions in my hands everywhere I went, always searching for that metal crank. I lived in that endlessly flat prairie terrain. And I grew farther and farther away from my true spirit.

I know some of this is inevitable. And even necessary. The directions for learning to drive are pretty important to follow. And, yeah, you want your doctor to follow the directions for the procedure she is going to perform. (You don't want to literally become loose parts!) But what percentage of the situations you find yourself in require these kinds of specific directions? Probably 10 percent. The remaining 90 percent is the stuff of varying possibilities. Of loose parts. Of our identities. And so who is best suited to make those decisions?

You are.

Being surrounded by trees—even if they are only on a block or in a park, even then!—gently reminds us that we have choices: we can shed the skins of peer pressure, parental pressure, societal pressure, and self-pressure and come closer to our centers. To our true selves.

This is not an easy process. It's tough to recognize which directions you do and don't want to follow. And it is equally as scary as it is exciting to follow the loose-parts model. I still struggle with both of these things. I have a feeling it is a lifelong process. And my hope is that the next time you are handed—quietly or aggressively—a set of directions and the tool to accomplish the job, you take a moment to yourself. Breathe in and breathe out. And in the space of that breath gather a loose part or two and take ownership of why and how to proceed.

We all have the right to experience this self-awareness. Whether we go up a mountain, or into the woods, a neighborhood park, a garden, or walk down a block planted with one flower; whether we follow a fox's footprints or a pigeon in the park—these are the moments when we give ourselves the opportunity to gather our own loose parts. And then—then!—we can go back to our parents, or peers, or teachers, or society at large with those ancient truths safely tucked inside. We can begin to swap out *following* directions for *choosing* them.

*   *   *   *   *

When you find that inner metal crank and begin to build your-self from the inside out, when you discover all of those glorious wild parts that together make you who you are, when you begin to carve your own mountains and rivers, when you begin to plant your own trees, when a tiny shoot bursts forth and a trickle of water begins to flow within your internal landscape—like Nate when he first climbed that mountain and me when I trekked down to the river—this is the moment you know it is worth it. This is the moment you begin to build your own fort. This is the moment you begin to find home.

GROW UP. BE SERIOUS.

TARA LAZAR

I have never gotten anywhere in my life by "being serious." Seriously.

Many people would like me to "grow up," namely my mother, the *What Not to Wear* devotee who worships the impeccably coiffed and platform-heel-addicted Stacy London, and who remains aghast over my penchant for Snoopy sweatshirts and rainbow tie-dyed tights.

As early as three years old, I remember my Italian grandmother dragging me to her salon, which oozed an odd combination of odors like hard-boiled eggs, toilet-bowl cleaner, and burning hair (an unmistakably *adult* smell which still makes me gag). While she perched underneath the brain-sucking alien dome the stylists called a hair dryer, she would lift her chin, flash a fake smile, and raise her voice an octave. "Tara, always be a *lady*. Always smile like a *lady*. Always say please and thank you like a *lady*. Men like ladies who know how to be *ladies*."

Really, Grandma? I had just barely squeaked past the Pampers and Pull-Ups era and already I had to be a lady? Dolled up like the Ultimate Grand Supreme contestants and sold off to a nursery school husband? Getting my hair yanked, teased, and bouffanted by sausage-fingered Marie Elena every Saturday morning? Um, I'll pass, thanks.

I wasn't even safe at school. I made good grades and hated to break any rules (unlike this book), but my teachers dragged me aside once a month to blow wisdom and coffee-cigarette breath in my face. "Tara, if only you applied yourself. You're always putting yourself on the back burner. Stop being so silly and *be serious*."

After imagining myself as a plump teakettle, quietly steaming on the rear range, I tried to grasp what they were saying. Not be silly? How is that even possible? How else do I shake off Bette Jean McDonald's cruel, cursing taunts or deflect my disappointment over Amy Solomon's sleepover snub? And how do I stay awake during algebra if I don't doodle "x" and "y" as stick-figure space invaders from Planet Integer?

To me, serious equaled boring. Serious was a college professor with elbow patches and a pipe, swirling philosophical sentiments about stuff I didn't understand, nor did I want to. *Why are we here? What is the purpose of life?*

Heck, the purpose of life is to live it. To enjoy it. And if I want to tell a joke about a priest, a rabbi, and an overweight electrician at (what others think is) a wildly inappropriate moment, I'm going to do it. As they say, you only live once, but you can tell the same joke over and over again.

Serious also equaled tension. Serious was a disagreement boiling over into a frothy argument, a spewing of unwelcome conflict requiring a resolution. I don't reach an answer by being serious. I relax. I let it meander through my mind. Then I let it go. I know that eventually, the kinks will unkink, even if I don't have the kink antidote at that exact moment. Tense times can always benefit from lightness and laughter.

Now that I'm a mother (and it's finally acceptable to wear a Snoopy sweatshirt), I see the pressure on kids to grow up as ever more present and annoying. I mean, why must a nine-year-old carry an iPhone, especially when *I* don't even own one? Who are they calling? With which movers and shakers are they sealing deals? Why are preschools naming themselves "Ivy Leaf," winking at parents with the coy suggestion that enrolling their toddlers will ensure future admission to Yale? Why do they sell size 6X girls' sweatpants with "H-A-W-T" scrawled across the tush? The kids just popped out of the womb and they're being rushed to mature faster than cheap wine.

We expect them to perform well at everything they attempt, but even adults aren't so well rounded. We can specialize in whatever field interests us, do the things we love in which we excel. (Like writing freakin' awesome essays for YA anthologies.) But children are enrolled in umpteen activities: soccer, baseball, softball, football, basketball, cheer, tap, jazz, ballet, piano, violin, tennis, swimming, fencing, spelunking, Girl Scouts, Boy Scouts, tae kwon do . . . deep breath . . . and if you have a few nanoseconds left, academic tutoring. And they're supposed to be flanked with metals, trophies, and letters of commendation for it all. I know eight-year-olds on traveling sports teams with practices three days a week and games so far-flung that they're covered by *Air & Space* magazine. They leave home before dawn and shuffle back at 10:00 PM to collapse (even before their worn-out parents). Geez! They're not professional athletes. Where's the time to play and explore without adult-imposed *rules*?

I suppose this is why the term "playdate" was invented. Kids can no longer run up the street, ring a doorbell, and traipse down to the stream with their bestie to collect tadpoles. Everyone's just too darn busy. You must schedule play, structure play, and monitor play. Even *play* has become *serious*. And what fun is that?

"Grow up and be serious" is the vampire sucking the lifeblood out of childhood, and he's not even Edward.

As a teen, you're probably feeling the activity anxiety too, trying to fill your college application with every extracurricular offering from ant farming to zither orchestra. The universities want to ensure they're accepting serious students, and to them, serious applicants are run-yourself-ragged after-school-club junkies. Frankly, young adults who are passionate about the *one* thing that brings them joy are the students who should be rewarded. Here's where being serious is useful—when you have a serious *passion*. It wins out in my book (and in *this* book, too).

But *not* being serious, instead being humorous and light, has always served me well, even when dealing with a serious disease. In 2009, I lost feeling in both feet and the numbness crept up my legs, making it nearly impossible to walk. When I was finally diagnosed with multiple sclerosis, I spotted a crafty little needlepoint in my neurologist's office, reminding me "laughter is the best medicine." I had to stop being so anxious and worried if I was going to live with this insidious thing. Because worrying never solves anything, it just stresses you out and makes you miss out on the here and now.

So when I roll down the sidewalk on my scooter, I ask the passing kids, "Do I have a sweet ride *or what*?" The answer is always "cool!" or "dude!" (even though, I'd like to point out, I'm a dudette). My cane is not a cane, but an author-chic accessory. When children wonder, "Why are you using a blue walker?" I tell them, "Because it's my favorite color." If someone tilts their head in pity, talks to me like I'm a lost, deaf kitten, and asks if I need help, I say, "Yes, please. Deposit one million dollars into my checking account. And I'll have fries with that. Thanks."

And when that person looks me over and responds, "I like your Snoopy sweatshirt," I know it's all going to be OK.

Seriously.

BOYS DON'T CRY

CHRIS LYNCH

It's all been said before, of course. But it bears a re-saying. Bears a lot of them, actually. Surely, the general consensus by now is that boys—big, small, and all—do cry, can cry, should cry.

But allow me to shamelessly piggyback, like so many others have, on the wonderful experience of the 2012 London Olympics for this moment.

Let's hear it for possibly the greatest collection of strong, fast, brave, accomplished, dazzling, *strapping*, medal-winning crybabies that have ever been propped up on podiums.

To borrow one of the great Irish phrasings: "On ya go, boyo!"

The phrase "man up" was not in use when I was a kid, as far as I'm aware. If it was I would have undoubtedly been even more emotionally ramshackle than I was. Because it has exactly the kind of macho-cool ring to it that I was a sucker for every time.

My father died just after my fifth birthday. I have two older brothers, but they were never of the bruising variety. Swimming and track types, they were effortlessly slim, almost willowy. Still are, really. Jerks.

The point is, I have no idea where I might have absorbed the idea of real men never crying, but I had swallowed it in one gulp, and it grew like a malignancy. Throughout the front-end years of my life, I put so much physical effort into not crying when the only reasonable response to something was to cry, I am sure it has shaved years off the back end. And since I am left with only the latter, I must admit I'm feeling pretty stupid about it now.

Maybe it was my obsession with sports. If Bobby Orr could go through a hundred knee operations and still have guys targeting his knees with those low checks the NHL seems to take notice of these days, who was I to shed a tear over a skinned knee? If Muhammad Ali could have his jaw broken halfway through his fight with Ken Norton (I must admit, I was furious to the *verge* of tears with Ali for taking Norton too lightly) and still keep fighting to the end, what pain would I ever have to match that? If Packers defensive back Willie Buchanon could endure a broken leg in 1973, come back to play in the savage NFL in 1974, break his leg *again* in 1975, then come back in 1976 and go on to have the best season of his career in 1978 ... well, fearless and tearless was certainly the only way to take on whatever life was going to bring me.

Which is not to say I never, ever, cried. There were occasions beyond even my control, of course. But on those occasions the shame of having wept completely overwhelmed the original pain that caused it. I wanted to take a baseball bat—there was always one handy—and bash my own crybaby self to death with the dishonor of the whole sorry episode. Only, my brain worked out that there would almost certainly be a stage before death that would, in fact, produce more tears, and, well, you can see where *that* would just be unacceptable.

Such is the logic that leaves me still here to discuss the matter.

Wherever I got the irrational macho ethos, I got it. I internalized it, nurtured it, committed to it.

In short, I was a chump. One should never be a chump.

But it has to go someplace. Crying is the emotional opening of a valve before the system explodes or shuts down entirely. So, if one is incapable of properly executing all of the handy, healthy options available, where does that pressure go?

Did I mention that I also have younger siblings?

My younger brother and I have had, in recent years, an informal understanding that whenever I have a public forum such as an interview I will make every effort to get an important message disseminated. That message is that I was an appalling, beastly older brother a great deal of the time. I informed him a year or so ago about such an interview with a publishing-industry magazine in which I had fulfilled that duty. He e-mailed me back something along the lines of, "Well, unless it was the *New Yorker* or something you still have a long way to go."

Thank goodness he can be funny now. But, was I, maybe, punishing him, venting on him, for whatever physical or emotional pains that I could not otherwise cope with? I don't have a certain answer, but I do know that I was pent up to the point where one option (tears) was no option and another (lashing out at a guy who was 99.8 percent innocent) was far, far too readily employed.

I was recently mentioning to my younger sister how this redemptive-confessional-public stocks thing is in place with our brother. Her response was something along the lines of, "Oh, I want in on that, starting right now."

So then, I was possibly even worse than I thought, though I remember more emotional-style cruelty with her than what I charmingly used to refer to as "slapstick" with my brother.

There was a common denominator, however. For my sadly undeveloped emotional range, somebody paid.

Is there any validity to the notion of delegating tears?

Crying by proxy?

I don't know, I don't know, I don't know.

But this I know:

Big boys absolutely cry.

Emotionally caged lunatic boys don't.

THE BOY/GIRL RULE

PAT SCHMATZ

When I was in sixth grade my class read a story about Baby X, and it changed the way I thought about the boy/girl rule forever. You know the rule: boys are like this, girls are like that. Boys wear this, say this, play this game. Girls wear something else, do something else, play a different game.

Over time the specifics have changed about what girls do and what boys do, and where they can overlap, but the boy/girl rule still exists. Even little children understand and follow it, and question people who don't.

Some of us don't care, and we break it every day. Most of us break it sometimes. Some of us never break it at all. And whether we mean to or not, almost all of us participate in enforcing the rule. Sometimes I catch myself enforcing it, and then I think about Baby X.

When Baby X was born, X's parents did not tell anyone if X was a boy or a girl. They knew, of course, and so did X's doctor. Nobody else. The relatives were upset because they didn't know whether to buy pink or blue, trucks or dolls.

By the time X went to school, X knew what X was, but X didn't tell and neither did X's parents. X used the principal's bathroom, but not even the principal knew if X was a boy or a girl. Sometimes

X lined up with the boys, and sometimes with the girls. X was all over the playground, playing all of the different games. X did whatever X was in the mood for that day.

Before reading about X, I ran into a lot of trouble around the boy/girl rule. One day in fifth grade, Glen Jackson looked at my feet and said, "Those are boys' boots." The way he looked at me, you'd think he'd caught me crawling around on my hands and knees eating dog poop, or maybe shooting endangered baby seals with a machine gun.

That wasn't the first time someone told me I was doing it wrong, or the last. People were always asking me, "Are you a boy or a girl?" The question alone let me know I was breaking the rule. The day I read the story of Baby X, I stopped thinking about me as wrong and started to wonder about the rule itself.

Like X, I knew what I was and my parents knew and the doctor knew and as for everyone else, why did it matter? Why did someone need to know if I was a boy or a girl before we could play ping-pong, or build a fort, or work on a math project?

I understood that males and females have biological differences. And of course, these become more important once we hit puberty. But when you're six, the boy/girl question is like getting asked for a driver's license before you can ride your tricycle past the neighbor's house. When I was a kid, it bothered me when people asked, because I could feel their disapproval. Even if it wasn't disapproval but just curiosity, it was a constant reminder that a rule existed and I was breaking it, just by being who I was.

The fiercest enforcers of the boy/girl rule weren't parents or teachers. They were other kids. Looking back, I can see that sometimes I was an enforcer, too. We enforced each other. The punishment for stepping out of line was often harsh and swift. From what I've seen, that has changed some ... in some places ... sometimes. But the boy/girl rule still exists, and the consequences for breaking it too much or too often or in particular ways are still pretty rough.

OK, I understand. Part of it is about being afraid people will think you're gay. Some of you *are* gay, and you don't hide it. Some of you don't know if you are or not. Some of you know you are and hide it, or worry that you are, or worry that other people will think you are. All of that worrying about being gay is changing, too—sometimes—in some places.

But even if you think being gay is the worst thing in the world—and no matter what anyone tells you, it's not—your activities or clothes don't make you gay or straight. Some straight men are beauticians, and some gay men play professional sports. Some lesbians are fashion models, and some straight women work in construction. Besides, back when everybody pretended that nobody was gay, the boy/girl rule was still there, still strict, and still enforced.

So what's really going on? Why do we need to identify everyone we meet as male or female—even tiny babies? And why do we all enforce this rule by immediately asking, if we can't tell by shoes or hairstyle or name, "Is that a boy or a girl?"

People who insist on breaking the rule can get in a lot of trouble. Sometimes they get punished so harshly by other kids that they can't take it and kill themselves. Sometimes, they don't have to kill themselves—the rule enforcers do it for them, or at least beat them so badly, either physically or emotionally, that they live in fear or run away to lose themselves in a city where nobody knows them.

You see a lot of press these days about bullying. Bullying is bad, sure, we all know that. But what if the bullying is really just rule enforcement? *Don't act like that. Don't wear those clothes. Don't look like you do.*

This book is about breaking rules. The boy/girl rule might work just fine for you. You might never worry about it, or even think about it. But maybe you want to break it once in a while and don't because you don't want the rule enforcers to get on you about it. Maybe you want to break it all the time but it's actually not safe, so you don't. Those are choices we all make, one situation at a time. For me, as one who often wants to break the rule but sometimes doesn't, it's important to be honest with myself about who I really am, and why I'm choosing to break it or not.

I loved the story of Baby X because not only did X break the rule, but when the other kids saw how free X was, they started to break it too. Everyone in X's class stopped enforcing the rule, so they all wore whatever clothes and played whatever games suited them.

When I was 11, that story was a revelation. The rules were the same, and the enforcers and consequences were the same, but I was different. The story of X set me free, at least in my own mind.

That's where freedom starts, and that's where change begins.

BE A MAN

ROB BUYEA

Like many boys, Owen couldn't remember when he was first told to be a man, but that expectation had been placed on him early. As terrified as he was as a seven-year-old at his Uncle Eddie's funeral, he didn't shed a tear. He was a smart boy. He knew he had to be tough. He knew he couldn't be scared—of anything—and he knew to forget about running to his mommy. He knew the last thing he ever wanted to be was a wimp. From the beginning, the message was clear, but just as it is for many boys, Owen's understanding of what it means to be a man was not.

In high school, Owen became a champion wrestler. Entering his senior year, he was solely focused on two goals: his team bringing home another league championship, and winning an individual state title. He worked his butt off. If his coach had asked him to run through a brick wall, he'd have done it. No question. He pushed himself through one grueling workout after another, no matter how tired he felt or how much he hurt. His coaches loved him. The girls loved him, his ripped body especially. Like so many boys, Owen had himself convinced that he was already a man. Heck, he thought he was *the* man. But he was wrong, and fortunately for Owen, there was Sammy.

Sammy had been alongside Owen every step of the way, but that didn't matter. He wasn't one of the tough guys. He wasn't a man. He was a cream puff, still on the junior varsity team as a senior. Most agreed that Sammy didn't even belong in a wrestling singlet. His man boobs spilled out during every match, and opponents and spectators would point and laugh like he was a circus freak attraction. At least the show never lasted long. Sammy was a turtle on his back. Once his opponent got him there, it was over.

Owen rarely paid attention to the junior varsity wrestlers, but on the rare occasion he did, he was always left wondering the same thing. Why didn't Sammy quit? It wasn't like he was ever going to wrestle varsity, or even win a match for that matter. The team didn't need him. But here again, Owen was wrong (as can be the case with adolescent boys. I know because I was one. There's so much to learn.). The varsity team's starting heavyweight was declared academically ineligible in late January, three days before their league championship dual meet. The only guy they had to turn to was Sammy.

It was a standing-room-only crowd for the highly anticipated showdown between the top two teams. The screaming fans and tightly packed bodies turned the gym into a sauna. You couldn't hear the person sitting next to you, never mind the coaches shouting instructions from the corner. The contest proved to be everything it was hyped up to be, with the back and forth battle going down to the wire.

Sammy stepped on the mat with everything on the line. The team had a five-point lead heading into his final match. If he could avoid being pinned then they would win. The rival spectators laughed like always when he lumbered out to the center, while *his* crowd grew eerily quiet.

Owen held his breath, but all hope leaked from his body. He felt weak. He, too, knew what was coming, and this time he was *not* wrong. It was no fairy-tale night. Sammy was slammed to his back and flattened in the first minute.

Owen was devastated. Losing wasn't something he was good at. The pain he felt was so intense and raw that it changed him. What others thought no longer mattered. He filled with anger. But here's the important part. He wasn't angry at Sammy. He was angry at himself. If he'd only given Sammy a chance maybe things could've been different. Sammy was there every day, but Owen had never helped him or even patted him on the back and told him, "Good job." Owen felt terrible. He blamed himself.

Later that night, as Owen was leaving, he heard a noise in a distant corner of the locker room. He walked over to discover Sammy sitting on a bench with his face in his hands. It was too much. Owen couldn't pretend to be what he wasn't, like he used to when he was a boy. No, this time he had to be honest about what he was feeling. He had to be a man. It took a lot more courage than being the tough guy did, but Owen moved closer and placed his hand on Sammy's back. "You showed great fight tonight, Sammy. You didn't let us down. Keep your head up."

Owen spent the next month helping Sammy every day after practice. It wasn't enough time to teach Sammy everything, but he was able to help him get better at fighting off a takedown, getting to his belly instead of going to his back, and hitting a roll from the bottom—a move that instantly reversed the top man and ended with Sammy in position for a pin. Five weeks after that devastating dual meet loss, the team traveled to the Class A Wrestling Championships, the first of their postseason tournaments. The top three place-finishers at each weight class would advance to the state qualifier.

Sammy started the day by facing the best wrestler in his weight class. Clearly outmatched, Sammy was slammed and pinned in just over 20 seconds. In his next match, however, Sammy was paired with Ben Storace—the same wrestler who had pinned him for the league championship five weeks earlier. Sammy was taken down, but not right away, and not to his back. He fought to his belly and found himself only losing by a score of 2–0 at the end of the first period. Then he survived the second period as well. Sure, he was losing by points, but Storace was sucking wind while Sammy still looked fresh. After all, Sammy had worked hard every day and even put in extra time. In the third and final period, with less than a minute to go, Sammy hit the roll. An exhausted Storace didn't have the strength or quickness to counter the move. Sammy came out on top and locked his arms around Storace. Storace fought but Sammy held on and squeezed. With just seconds remaining, the referee slapped the mat, signaling a pin for Sammy. He had won his first match ever. Owen, who had been screaming his head off the entire time, rushed the mat and hugged Sammy in celebration—and for the first time since he was a little boy, his eyes filled with tears.

Owen dominated his competition that day and was voted the tournament's Most Outstanding Wrestler. Two weeks later he won the state championship and was again voted the tournament's Most Outstanding Wrestler. It was something he had dreamed about for a long time, yet none of it felt as special as when Sammy won that match.

After graduating from college Owen found himself teaching and coaching a high school wrestling team. Thanks to Sammy, he knew he wanted to spend his life making a difference in other's lives. Thanks to Sammy, he grew to understand that while being hard and tough helped win wrestling championships, it took more than that to be a man.

DRESS APPROPRIATELY

MARGO RABB

I have a recurring fantasy: the famous artist Georgia O'Keeffe has been nominated to be on TLC's hit TV show *What Not to Wear*. The hosts, Stacy and Clinton, begin to mock Georgia in their typical way: they criticize her black-and-white wardrobe, her penchant for men's shoes, her head scarf that resembles a nun's habit, and her Amish-style black hat.

"Color," Clinton sighs. "Your complexion *cries* for color. Why would an artist choose such a dreary palette of neutrals?"

"You want people to meet you and think, 'Famous Person,' not 'Crazy Old Art Lady,'" Stacy says.

What does Georgia tell them?

"Go to hell," Georgia says. She waltzes out of the TV studio in her men's oxfords; the long tail of her head scarf flaps in the wind. She hops on her motorcycle and speeds off to New Mexico, where she can wear whatever she likes, in peace.

I've loved fashion as long as I can remember—a love that I've often tried to forget. I've tried to convince myself it was superficial to care. It always seemed that there were two sides of myself at odds with each other: the side of me that copied out "It is only with the heart that one can see rightly; what is essential is invisible to the eye," from *The Little Prince* and used it as my senior quote in my high school yearbook, and the side that saved up my after-school earnings for months so I could buy a pair of black suede shoes that I'd worshipped through the window of a shop on Eighth Street. The truth is, I still believe both things at once: the most essential, important things *are* invisible, but the ability to express one's true self is an art. Creating beauty—be it through paintings, poems, or fashion—is an essential part of being human. And mustering the guts to be confident in those creations is one of the hardest things we ever learn to do.

Fashion hasn't always been a source of pleasure for me. I remember the first time I longed for clothes as a way to fit in. I was 11, and my sister and I had received "campership funds" to attend a summer camp in upstate New York. A lot of wealthy kids went to this camp, and they wore an unofficial uniform of Izod shirts, designer jeans, Tretorn tennis sneakers, and blucher moccasins from L.L. Bean. Before camp, I wouldn't have recognized a Tretorn or blucher if it had bonked me on the head. Still, I felt embarrassed that I didn't own these things, and that I had never even heard of them before.

One night at camp, I dressed up for a dance in my favorite outfit: a pastel yellow polo shirt and cropped lavender jeans from Fabulous Julie's, a discount store in Flushing, with striped socks and clunky, no-name sneakers.

I felt pretty good in my outfit. More than good. The yellow polo and lavender pants were such pretty colors, and I'd kept them in good shape, immediately hand-washing any spaghetti sauce stain or stray smudge of dirt that appeared. I felt so good in this outfit that when I walked by an older, popular girl named Beth, I waved at her.

"You look like a spaz!" she said.

As she said that, the words took a long time—too long—to register; in fact I had been so certain that she was going to compliment me that I cheerfully chirped, "Thanks!" before what she'd said sunk in. When the words finally did sink in, I was flooded with 10 different kinds of shame. *Spaz.* I froze.

Beth chuckled to herself, shook her head, and walked off.

Back home in Queens, I begged my parents for bluchers and Tretorns, though they were out of our budget. My mom finally buckled and bought them. What was cool in the 1980s at Upper East Side and suburban prep schools, though, seemed ugly and dorky at my junior high school, J.H.S. 125.

If I'd appeared on a 1980s version of *What Not To Wear*, who knows what Stacy and Clinton would've said to me, whether they would've embraced Tretorns or not. I do know that being on that show would feel endlessly humiliating to me. Reality shows seem harmless through the veneer of the TV, but if you think of what actually is going on—gathering a group of family and friends to talk about you behind your back, to point out all the embarrassing things you wear and to laugh at your appearance in front of an audience of over a million—it's actually public shaming. The clothes we wear should never be a source of shame, and the problem with both *What Not to Wear* and the school pressure to wear certain things to fit in is that it assumes that there's something wrong with you if you don't own the "right" items in the first place. There's something wrong with you, period. There's something that needs to be fixed.

What real fashion and style are about is discovering and declaring that there's nothing wrong with you. There's nothing that needs to be fixed. You are perfect exactly the way you are. Our uniqueness is what makes us human, and though we often suppress that uniqueness to fit in, we need to learn to do the opposite. To show who you are, to express yourself to the world.

"Who is this 'yourself,'?" you ask. Ah, that's the problem. I used to think that when I grew up I'd finally figure it out. The truth is, I still haven't figured it out—not completely. As soon as I think I've figured it out, something changes drastically in my life and alters who I am. That's what life is—it's always changing; it never stops. Our styles change as our lives change.

Fashion's true pioneers had the guts and self-confidence to stray from the mainstream and to break the rules: Coco Chanel popularized pants and ran her own business when few women dared to. "I gave women a sense of freedom," she said once. "I gave them back their bodies: bodies that were drenched in sweat, due to fashion's finery, lace, corsets, underclothes, padding." The writer Gore Vidal said, "Style is knowing who you are, what you want to say, and not giving a damn." The designer Marc Jacobs loves to wear women's perfume, skirts, and dresses. He recently wore a see-through black lace dress to a Metropolitan Museum of Art gala with white boxers underneath. "I'm not one who has this distinction between masculine and feminine," he said. "I don't concern myself with good taste or bad taste when I get dressed. Convention to me is just boredom!"

Clothes are not only clothes. They're how we present ourselves to the world. They reveal our personalities, who we are and who we strive to be. They can enlighten and deceive. You can look rich with clothes from Goodwill or a dress you sewed yourself, or you can be a billionaire in worn jeans and a Hanes T-shirt. Of course, there are places to dress appropriately—college admissions interviews, job interviews, offices, and funerals, among them—but the rest of the time, there are no rules. If you want to wear a squirrel hat that you made yourself, that's great. Or a tutu, even if you're a football player. Or combat boots if you're a ballerina. Or . . . anything.

I'd like to pitch this show to a TV network: Two stylists travel around the country and peek inside people's closets. "Look at this!" they say at the handmade squirrel hat with a matching tuxedo. "This is so cool and different." We need more squirrel hats, and girls in boys' shoes, and football players in tutus, and men in lace dresses with boxer shorts underneath. There are parts of us we'll show to the world today, but not tomorrow. Next year and last year and 10 years from now new parts of us come and go, become buried and resurface. We need to keep on mustering the guts to show all the different sides of ourselves, to try on new sides. We need to admit that we never stop growing and changing and that we always need courage to face the world.

THERE ARE FIRM RULES IN LIFE

THANHHA LAI

like rules. I have no problem following them. Why not? They seem designed to bring order to life. I like order. But nothing is that easy. Rules, by inherent nature, are tricky. For every rule, there's an equally persuasive counter-rule, much like the law that says for every action, there's a reaction.

For example:

1. Follow your bliss. Who wouldn't want to do this? You can hear rah-rah music swelling in your head as you dash out the door, jump into a convertible, and head toward the coast to pursue your dreams. But here's this pesky other rule: nothing is guaranteed. So months, years, decades later, what if you must admit that your bliss has no correlation with your capabilities? Then is it time to follow the job market? Music does not swell for this rule, ever. But that doesn't mean it's not worth following.

2. So you grow up, be responsible. Entire nations are built on this rule alone. You get into the right college, finesse the right job, buy the right house, acquire the right car. Then one day you realize you don't want any of these things as much as you want to (drumroll) . . . follow your bliss.

3. Of course you turned responsible in the first place because you listened to your elders. They, the wiser, quieter crowd, supposedly know what's worth sacrificing for because they've lived longer. Then another day you realize that not every elder is worth listening to.

4. But you can't quite drop everything and follow your bliss again because there's this voice in your head that dictates *don't quit*. You take the thought one more step and feel even more stumped: don't quit following your dreams, or don't quit being responsible?

5. Of course, you want to do the right thing, but what if the wrong thing is right for you?

By now, if you're still with me, you're probably thinking, WHAT? That one word, WHAT? (always in caps, with a question mark) essentially sums up every rule in life. If you want to get philosophical, WHAT? sums up life itself.

WHAT am I rambling about? (Huge drumroll please).

There is no rule to follow; there is no rule to break. You follow and break rules just through the act of living. At times you'll be conscious of the rules, but I bet most of the time you'll just be trying to figure out the next step that allows you to walk a bit taller.

So follow your bliss, if that's what you need to do right now. Later, you might want to retract your bliss and change course. No rule says you can't.

Do what feels right, right now. When it no longer feels right, stop.

Now I sound like a Zen guru on a mountaintop. You might be thinking life is much more complicated than the la-di-da approach of "the rule is there is no rule." Actually, life is essentially la-di-da, if you let it be.

Imagine yourself floating or sinking or rushing or fighting your way through life, and rules pop up as little life jackets that you grab or discard according to your immediate needs. Of course the trick is knowing when to grab or discard which rule and for how long. Most likely you won't get it right the first time, or even the 10th, but with grace and practice, you will.

I hope that you end up floating a lot. It makes the act of grabbing or discarding much more enjoyable.

DON'T LET THE NEW WORLD CHANGE YOU

MITALI PERKINS

My parents were among the first Bengalis to raise children in the United States. Thanks to their bold move from Kolkata, India, to a California suburb, the three of us Bose girls were conscious of eyes scrutinizing our every move. To shield our family from disrepute, three rules were made clear from the start.

Confession: I shattered all three before graduating from college.

Rule Number One: You will become a doctor or engineer.

Bengali is the fifth most commonly spoken language on the planet. There are gazillions of us here, there, and everywhere, but apparently the news of a student declaring an artsy college major spreads through the diaspora faster than cholera.

Even if you scoff at your parents' fear of feeding the gossip chain, guilt keeps you from stomping on rule number one with gusto. They came here for *you* to have a better life, remember? Do you think they *enjoy* questions about accents, forehead dots, saris, and so on?

I broke rule number one by declaring a political science major, and I totally decimated it some years later by choosing to write fiction. For young readers, no less.

Here's the irony: my mother has morphed into my loudest fan. Her Facebook feed now reads like a streaming advertisement for books by Mitali Bose Perkins. My 80-something father is just as bad, but he doesn't have a Facebook account. Not yet, anyway.

Rule Number Two: You will marry a Bengali guy. He, too, will be a doctor or engineer. Oh, and your parents will select him.

This one was easy to ignore because I was a third daughter. By the time I came of age, our exhausted parents didn't ask many questions. There wasn't even a feeble attempt to arrange my marriage. The guy I chose for myself was educated, employed, and came from a decent family. Who cared that he wasn't Indian? He wasn't in jail, like one of the questionable dudes who had pursued my sisters.

Rule Number Three: You are, and always will be (at least in this incarnation), a Hindu.

Rule number three was the hardest to break. My identity was fundamentally Bengali—I enjoyed being a thoroughbred in this new world of mutts. I spoke the language, I cooked with mustard seed and cumin, I could drape, fold, and tuck a sari—I was brown and proud of it. Wasn't Hinduism intrinsically bound up in who I was?

But then a friend died in a senseless car accident, and I began asking the big questions. I read philosophy, studied world religions, and argued into the wee hours with friends who disagreed with each other when it came to questions of faith.

Someone suggested I read the New Testament in the Christian Bible. *That white people's book?* I thought, but I picked it up. I started with the Gospel of Mark. There, in a series of simply told stories, I discovered a Jewish guy with Middle Eastern values that resonated with my culture of origin. I read on, swept off my feet by his Sermon on the Mount, tenderness with outcasts, empowerment of women and the poor.

Could I take Jesus as my guru and remain Bengali? I thought. *What would such a decision mean to my parents?* This time, I really was worrying about bringing shame and dishonor to the family name. I read *Mere Christianity,* and C. S. Lewis's compelling arguments further confirmed my desire to follow Jesus. Soon, after months of conversation and reflection, that's what I became: a Bengali follower of Jesus, fusing a new religious and cultural identity.

Here's the shocker: despite the mostly negative reaction in the Bengali community, my parents staunchly supported me. Their strong love for me overcame their fear of shame. Soon, it was clear to everyone—including me—that they were celebrating my vocation, my marriage, *and* my faith with heads held high.

I had broken the rules, but not their hearts.

These days, when immigrant families ask for insight into surviving the generational battle, I point to my parents as shining stars. "Cultures always collide, clash, and change," I say. "But check out those two old people: the rule of Love endures forever."

ME FIRST

LYNDA MULLALY HUNT

He didn't look like he'd play the part of someone else's savior. His own mother called him a hood. At 17, he had long hair, a history of fighting, some brushes with the law, and a school-wide reputation among the teachers. I had heard that he'd grow up to be nothing but an inmate.

And yet, every day when I came out of first grade, there he was. Leaning against the wall, hands stuffed into the pockets of his black peacoat. He'd smile in that lopsided way—only on the right. Flipping his head to the side to toss the sweep of hair from his eyes. "Hey, Lulu," he'd say. His nickname for me since I've had a memory. As a toddler, I called him "Keke" because I couldn't say my big brother's name, Ricky.

Ricky was 11 when I was born. That made 5 children in the family, and he carried more responsibility than any 11-year-old should have to. Soon after I arrived, he became the man of the house, as my mother had told my father to leave.

Our mum was funny and charming and had the heart of a child. She was intelligent and cunning and was able to pull off things that few others could. She was brave and focused. When moments of clarity and energy came on, she was able to move mountains when it came to the big picture. One such example was moving us from a literal slum in a depressed area to renting a condemned (but pest-free) building "under the radar" in one of the best school districts in the state. However, in the day-to-day caring for a family, she was too lost in her own pain. She was unable to be the parent that her heart wanted her to be. This mother needed to be mothered even more than her children did.

So, Ricky took care of some of the big things. He helped to make decisions. He stayed up all night to paint rooms by himself or fix things around the house. He went to the Laundromat with my mum every week. He helped look out for our special needs brother and often propped up my mother. And he added humor and laughter to our family. And what did I learn from all of this?

I learned that there is a difference between an "older brother" and a "big brother" and Ricky has always been the latter. The big things mattered, but it was also in the millions of little things over thousands of days. Frying me an egg if I was hungry. Spending his own money to be sure I'd have Christmas presents under the tree. Taking me to the children's museum and out to lunch. I remember him holding a handful of change at McDonald's and, while he counted it, asking me if I wanted something else. I said no, but his face was earnest. "I can get you another burger if you're hungry. Are you sure?" he asked.

Not to say we didn't disagree, as all people who love each other do. One day, when a caller asked for my mother on the phone, I replied, "She can't talk right now. She's building a pedestal for Ricky in the basement." And then I hung up.

But I always knew he was my flesh-and-blood guardian angel.

I got sick a lot when I was young. Sick with asthma, which would escalate quickly. I was admitted to the pediatric floor 22 times in my kindergarten year alone. My mother would tell Ricky that I was sick, and he would be the one to put his ear to my chest to see if he could hear the fluid and wheezing. I still remember the relief I felt when he'd intervene and the smell of his hair when he did this.

On one visit to the emergency room, Ricky carried me through the automatic double doors. I was limp and only semiconscious. The nurse pointed her chin toward the room full of orange chairs and told him that there would be a wait. Glancing over at the crowded waiting room, looking down at my chapped lips and pale face, feeling my labored breathing, he told her that I was sick. That I could not wait.

She snapped at him, saying that we'd wait our turn like everyone else. As he held me in his arms, the memory of our brother, Michael Eric, coming to the hospital a few years earlier must have rung in his head. How Michael Eric had had pneumonia and asthma. How he had gone into respiratory failure. And how he never came home again.

His grip on me tightened. At first, he shifted his weight but then stood firm under the fluorescent lights in front of that desk and yelled, "No! This is *my* little sister. We are *not* going to wait. Now, you move your ass and you get a goddamn doctor out here to help her." He choked on his words. "My little *sister*—can't *breathe*."

Security closed in. Other nurses approached, angry that he'd sworn at their colleague. A doctor came over and touched my face. He then waved to another staff member to get us into a room. Security was poised to remove Ricky, but he was ultimately brought in to sit with me.

Years later, after he went to the University of Connecticut, he'd come home to play classical music for me; he said I should know about things like that. And then there were the tennis lessons, which really amounted to Ricky chasing tennis balls over the fences.

Sometimes, he'd return from college to take me to church on Sunday. I got the same chill every time I watched him find the right pages for me. The feel of his hand on my shoulder was the only positive human contact I had had while he was at college. And he was never pushy about his faith—it was quiet and strong.

I may have been the only kid in town who looked forward to going to church.

I've long had a wish, though. A wish that Ricky had had his own "Ricky." I had him, but he didn't really have anyone. With all my heart, I wish he had, because I can't think of anyone that deserved it more. Eventually, Ricky did end up in court. He has stood before judges many times, having been in the system for years now. As an attorney.

Close friends have commented that it must be sad for me to never really have had a father I could trust and depend on. My head knows that's true, but my heart has never had to agree. For wrapped inside that peacoat—and now a suit and tie—is Ricky. My big brother, one of my very best friends, and the only dad figure I'll ever know.

Or ever need.

Yes, Ricky was special. Still is. But after all these things that I've already cited—and there are more—the two best things he ever did?

First, he married Jill, who may not be a sister by blood but is one in all the ways that matter far more. I couldn't love her any more if we had grown up together.

The other?

Ricky has always lit up when I've walked into the room.

I have memories of this at the ages of four and eight and eighteen. He does that even now. And although my childhood may have been lacking in other ways, was I ever lucky that I had him—for just brightening when he saw me sent such a powerful message. I stood taller. I felt whole. I knew he expected much of me, so I expected it of myself.

What if Ricky had not broken this rule of "Me first"?

I would not have learned that life is about human connection. That you don't need a bunch of people—just one that you know you can always count on. His attentiveness taught me that although the words "I love you" are wonderful to hear, love is about action. It's about being there even when it isn't convenient. It's in the doing, not in the feeling.

I know from experience that the best way to distract yourself from your own problems is to help someone else with theirs. I've also learned how lifting up someone else lifts you up right along with them. Sharing of ourselves in this way is the best humanity has to offer. And you never know which gesture will make the difference—and how far-reaching it can turn out to be.

Ricky's generosity in prioritizing me has affected the person, wife, parent, student, teacher, friend, citizen, and author that I have become. I do hope that all of these roles have helped me help others. But if I've had any impact, it's because of that "hood" in the peacoat.

Watching Ricky fight for his happiness—and for mine—also taught me about surviving the tough times. You have to let go. Have faith. Know the kinds of chances to take. Be honest. Look at the world and the people around you. But remember to look inward too; don't be easily led by others. Do the right thing even when it's hard. *Pay attention.* Take care of the ones who love you. And remember that, when it comes to life and love and expectations and writing and a thousand other things, it's not about merely holding on.

It's all in the reaching.

ACKNOWLEDGMENTS

Over the course of my teaching career, my students have taught me immeasurably more than I've ever taught them. I'm grateful to all my students—past and present—for the vulnerability, courage, and hope you show every day of your lives as you seek to grow and learn. Thanks for sharing your lives with me. This book exists because you cared passionately about seeking something more than the status quo. Together, we learned to break these rules.

My agent, Ammi-Joan Paquette, heard about this project in its initial stages; her excitement about what this book could become, as well as her help to create, guide, and sustain it, was inspiring. JLA, you are not only an incredibly savvy editor and coach, but you're also a person who evidences kindness and joy in small ways and big. Thank you so very much for being who you are.

The authors within this book put aside other important writing projects, jobs, teaching concerns, and various other responsibilities to craft these powerful essays. Without compensation and without a guarantee, you were vulnerable and passionate enough to speak out against rules in profound ways. I wish I had had all of your words when I was growing up, and I am deeply grateful that you've offered them here. Thank you for supporting the work of the Children's Defense Fund through this book. Corresponding and working with you all has been a dream come true.

Our editor at Chicago Review Press, Lisa Reardon, has been such a joy to work with, learn from, and correspond with about all issues big and small. Lisa, your enthusiasm for the *Break These Rules* project from start to finish has been deeply encouraging and meaningful.

Mom and Dad—Harry and Kathy Reynolds—you have always tried to teach us to follow our hearts rather than what society demands. Thanks for your belief that journeys matter more than money and status. Thanks for sharing your faith and your unconditional love. And brothers! Chris, Mike, Bryan, and Matthew: could a guy ever be luckier than to sit alongside you watching movies like *The Wedding Planner* and camping in the woods laughing with great giddiness? And to Susan and Wendell Anderson: in-laws who lovingly believe in the power of books to change lives and inspire us deeply. Thanks for your belief in my journey as a writer and our journey as a family.

To the friends who offer such steadfast challenge, resolve, and vision to break the rules to see what might be possible: Phil and Kate Andersen, Wade Austin, Paul and Diana Gant, Ryan and Kelly Ribelin, Al and Lucy Rycroft, and James Simister.

To the teachers who modeled the kind of resistance to status quo thinking that shocked my soul into a new kind of hope: Mike Baxer, Paul Borgman, Marilyn Cochran-Smith, Ann Cummins, Mike Dunn, Robert Looney, Nancy Paxton.

To John Robinson—for every day we sat on the "front porch" as we welcomed students into Room 106. You taught me to see the purpose of education as revolutionary, the goal of our existence to be radical and compassionate and deeply alive and connected to one another, to literature, to love. Wild One, you never stop believing in that most dangerous thing of all: hope. And you show me how to believe, too.

My wife, Jennifer, listened and offered ideas and insights during every step of this project's development. Her unbridled enthusiasm for all things that buck the status quo as well as her passion for social justice fueled the creation of this book. Jen, your love and passion are remarkable, and no matter what life throws our way, you take it as oxygen and you glow brighter. Thanks for the fire of your heart. Thanks for letting me walk beside you on this journey.

ABOUT THE CONTRIBUTORS

Ever since he coauthored a Howard Cosell parody in third grade, **Chris Barton** has been drawn toward writing as a community activity, and there's no better place in the world for that than Austin, Texas. In the dozen or so years since he was a fledgling in the local children's literature scene, Chris has written picture books (*The Day-Glo Brothers: The True Story of Bob and Joe Switzer's Bright Ideas and Brand-New Colors* (Charlesbridge 2009), about the guys who invented those colors, and *Shark vs. Train* (Little, Brown 2010), about, um, a shark versus a train) and the young adult nonfiction thriller, *Can I See Your I.D.?: True Stories of False Identities* (Dial 2011). He's also considered himself lucky to get to do what he loves alongside Austin's terrific authors, illustrators, librarians, and booksellers—and to count those same folks among his friends. He's also the dad to two brilliant, inquisitive, and (yes!) curious boys whom he hopes will feel free to go to college if and when it's right for them.

Josh Berk is the author of several books for teens and young readers, including *The Dark Days of Hamburger Halpin* (Knopf 2010), named a 2010 best book for teens by *Kirkus Reviews* and Amazon .com. Other titles include *Guy Langman: Crime Scene Procrastinator* (Knopf 2012), as well as the Lenny and the Mikes series (Knopf) of baseball-themed mysteries. He has previously been a journalist, a poet, a playwright, and a guitarist (mostly in bands known for things other than fine guitar-playing). Josh comes from a family of librarians, and he is currently a library director. He lives in Bethlehem, Pennsylvania. Visit him online at www .joshberkbooks.com. Don't visit him in person due to his army of attack Boston terriers.

Lisa Burstein is a tea seller by day and a writer by night. She received her MFA in fiction from the Inland Northwest Center for Writers at Eastern Washington University. She lives in Portland, Oregon, with her very patient husband, a neurotic dog, and two cats. She is the author of the young adult contemporary novels *Pretty Amy* (Entangled 2012), and *Dear Cassie* (Entangled 2013).

Rob Buyea taught third and fourth graders in Bethany, Connecticut, for six years before moving to Northfield Mount Hermon School in Massachusetts, where he lives with his wife and three daughters, teaches biology, and coaches wrestling. *Because of Mr. Terupt* (Yearling 2011), his first novel, was selected as an E. B. White Read-Aloud Award Honor Book, a Cybils Award finalist, and has been named to numerous state award lists. Rob spends his summers at Cape Cod enjoying family adventures, entertaining friends, and writing. You can visit him at www.robbuyea.com.

Leslie Connor writes books for children of all ages. Her work spans the genres from picture books to young adult novels, from historical fiction to contemporary themes. Her award-winning titles include a picture book, *Miss Bridie Chose a Shovel* (Houghton Mifflin 2004), and young adult novels *Waiting for Normal* (Katherine Tegen Books 2010) and *Crunch* (Katherine Tegen Books 2012). Leslie says her writing days begin *not* at her desk but on the hiking trails near her home. "I start to put my head into my work and it's amazing how details can rise during a march through the ferns. When I get home, I pour a pot of tea, sit down, and begin." Leslie's advice to writers is: write what you can't ignore! (Chances are good that others will be interested too.) Leslie lives in a little house in the big Connecticut woods with her husband and three grown children (who come home in between their own adventures) and three rescued writing dogs.

Sayantani DasGupta was never very good at following rules. She trained as a pediatrician but ended up teaching in graduate school. She also writes for children and young adults. She writes academically about race, gender, and education but also writes a lot for websites like Adios, Barbie and From the Mixed Up Files of Middle Grade Authors. And she watches way more America's Next Top Model than really anyone should. Besides secretly watching television and hanging out with her 10- and 8-year-old kids, Sayantani is also the coauthor of *The Demon Slayers and Other Stories: Bengali Folk Tales* (Interlink Publishing Group 1994), the author of a memoir called *Her Own Medicine: A Woman's Journey from Student to Doctor* (Fawcett 1999), and the coeditor of a collection of women's illness narratives called *Stories of Illness and Healing: Women Write Their Bodies* (Kent State University Press 2007). She is working on a fantasy adventure novel for middle graders based on Bengali folktales and another for teens based on a futuristic retelling of the Indian epic *The Mahabharata*. Sayantani is represented by the wonderful Erin Murphy of Erin Murphy Literary Agency.

Carl Deuker currently teaches in the Northshore School District outside of Seattle. He is the author of *On the Devil's Court* (Little, Brown 2008), *Heart of a Champion* (Little, Brown 2007), *Night Hoops* (Graphia 2009), *Painting the Black* (HarperTeen 2009), *High Heat* (HarperTeen 2005), *Runner* (Graphia 2007), and *Gym Candy* (Graphia 2008). *On the Devil's Court* was YA Book of the Year in South Carolina; *Heart of a Champion* was named Book of the Year in Nebraska, Pennsylvania, and Tennessee; *Night Hoops* won in Nebraska; and *High Heat* also won the Golden Sower Award in

Nebraska. Carl shares, "My father died when I was three years old, so my sister Beth and I were raised by our mother, Marie. I lived all my childhood in Redwood City, a suburb of San Francisco. I attended good schools with good teachers and made good grades, but I don't think it was school that first pointed me toward a writing career. As a child, I'd often take out my Tinkertoys and start building. I'd work my way out of my bedroom and down the hall toward the living room. As I laid out my toys, my mind would be going. Sometimes it was cowboys and Indians, sometimes cops and robbers. All the time I'd be making up stories. I was an OK athlete—good enough to make teams but not good enough to play much. I spent most of my time watching my more skilled teammates. But that wasn't the worst thing for a future writer either. More time to imagine. For years I wrote movie and book reviews for a small Seattle alternative newspaper. Then one day I thought to myself: Stop kidding yourself. If you want to write fiction, write fiction. So I did, and with luck and help from editor Ann Rider, have published eight young adult novels, all of which have had a sports theme. My goal now is to keep writing.

Kathryn Erskine was born in the Netherlands and grew up in six countries, attending eight schools and four universities. She spent 15 years as a lawyer before deciding to break the rule of having a safe and steady career and instead began writing for young people. Her first book, *Quaking* (Philomel 2007), was an American Library Association (ALA) Top Ten Quick Pick for Reluctant Young Adult Readers. *Mockingbird* (Philomel 2010) won the 2010 National Book Award for Young People's Literature, and *The Absolute Value of Mike* (Philomel 2011) won a Crystal Kite Award. She has many more novels in the works, including *Facing Freedom* (Scholastic 2013). Her books tend to cover weighty topics but include warmth and humor, making difficult issues approachable. She gives workshops and presentations on writing, and she frequently visits schools. When she's not reading or writing, Kathryn loves walking, exploring, traveling, playing card and board games, learning languages (or anything, really), and spending time with family and friends. She can be reached online at www.kathrynerskine.com, kathyerskine .wordpress.com, and on Facebook as Kathy Erskine.

Lynda Mullaly Hunt has marched to the beat of her own drummer since she learned to march. She has bucked low expectations. She has rocked the boat. She has always believed that rules aren't necessarily made to be broken, but their merits should be considered before blindly following. She is the author of both *One for the Murphys* and *Alphabet Soup* (Both from Nancy Paulsen Books/ Penguin 2012 and 2014). Lynda loved being a teacher and scenario writing coach for almost 10 years. Presently, she is a retreat director for Society of Children's Book Writers and Illustrators (SCBWI). She loves watercolor painting, juggling beanbags as well as schedules, and still likes to create a bit of harmless mischief now and then. She lives with her husband, two teenagers, impetuous beagle, and beagle-loathing cat.

Under the right circumstances **Mike Jung** actually can be kind of a loudmouth, but those circumstances are kind of rare. He's a father, husband, library professional, semicompetent ukulele player, former art student, reformed crazy cat person, Internet despot, Northern California resident, and (obviously) madly introverted author. Mike's first novel, *Geeks, Girls, and Secret Identities*, was published in October 2012 by Arthur A. Levine Books / Scholastic.

A. S. King is the author of *Ask the Passengers* (Little, Brown 2012) and *Everybody Sees the Ants* (Little, Brown 2011), a highly acclaimed 2012 ALA Top Ten Best Fiction for Young Adults book and Andre Norton Award nominee, and the Edgar Award nominated, 2011 Michael L. Printz Award Honor Book *Please Ignore Vera Dietz* (Ember 2012). She is also the author of the ALA Best

Books *The Dust of 100 Dogs* and the upcoming *Reality Boy* (Little, Brown 2013). After a decade living self-sufficiently and teaching literacy to adults in Ireland, she now provides literacy outreach for teens throughout the United States and lives in the Pennsylvania woods with her husband and children.

Thanhha Lai was born in Vietnam and immigrated to the United States at the end of the war in 1975. She currently lives in New York City. Her novel for young adults, *Inside Out & Back Again* (HarperCollins 2011) explores the event of being rescued in 1975 during an operation led by the USS *Kirk*. In 2011, she won the National Book Award for Young People's Literature for this novel.

Tara Lazar loves composing witty bios that make her sound interesting, but often fails. She is the author of *The Monstore* (Aladdin 2013), a picture book you cannot return or exchange, just like the monsters in the story. *I Thought This Was a Bear Book* and *Little Red Gliding Hood,* loosely based on her figure skating years, are forthcoming from Aladdin / Simon & Schuster and Random House. There are more wacky antics on her blog, including author interviews and book giveaways. Tara lives in New Jersey with her husband, two daughters, and 4,892 stuffed animals (all which she won from crane machines on the boardwalk). Follow along at your own risk: www.taralazar.com.

Natalie Dias Lorenzi is 100 percent Natalie, and her husband, Davide Lorenzi, is 100 percent Davide. Together they make up two wholes. Natalie is a school librarian and a teacher who specializes in teaching English to second-language learners. She is also a freelance writer and the author of *Flying the Dragon* (Charlesbridge 2012), a middle grade novel for children.

Chris Lynch is the author of several books for young readers, including Michael L. Printz Award Honor Book *Freewill*

(HarperCollins 2001), National Book Award finalist *Inexcusable* (Atheneum 2007), and the four-book Vietnam series for middle grade readers (Scholastic Press). He teaches in the low-residency MFA creative writing program at Lesley University, and divides his time between Scotland and Massachusetts.

Wendy Mass is the *New York Times* best-selling author of 11 novels for young people (which have been translated into 13 languages and nominated for 46 state book awards), including *A Mango-Shaped Space* (Little, Brown 2005), which was awarded the Schneider Family Book Award by the American Library Association, *Leap Day* (Little, Brown 2006), the Twice Upon a Time fairy tale series (Scholastic Press), *Every Soul a Star* (Little, Brown 2009), *11 Birthdays* (Scholastic Paperbacks 2010), *Heaven Looks a Lot Like the Mall* (Little, Brown 2008), *Jeremy Fink and the Meaning of Life* (Little, Brown 2008), and *Finally* (Scholastic Paperbacks 2011). Her most recent books are *The Candymakers* (Little, Brown 2011) and *13 Gifts* (Scholastic Press 2011). Wendy wrote the storyline for an episode of the television show *Monk*, entitled "Mr. Monk Goes to the Theatre," which aired during the show's second season. She tells people her hobbies are hiking and photography, but really they're collecting candy bar wrappers and searching for buried treasure with her metal detector. She lives with her family in New Jersey.

Neesha Meminger was born in Punjab, India, grew up in Toronto, Canada, and now lives in New York City. She holds an undergraduate degree in film and media, and an MFA in creative writing. In its debut year, Neesha's first novel, *Shine, Coconut Moon* (Margaret K. McElderry Books 2010), was listed on the Smithsonian's Notable Books for Children list and made the New York Public Library's "Stuff for the Teen Age—Top 100 Books." *Shine, Coconut Moon* was also nominated for the American Library Association's Best Books for Young Adults and the online Cybils Award.

Jazz in Love (Ignite Books 2011), Neesha's second novel for young adults, was also nominated for a Cybils Award and was selected as a Top 40 book for teens by the Pennsylvania School Librarians' Association. In addition, *Jazz in Love* made Bookslut's Recommended Summer Reads list in its debut year. *Into the Wise Dark* (Ignite Books 2012), a time-travel novel featuring the sunken land mass known as Kumari Kundam, is Neesha's third novel for Young Adults. For more information, visit Neesha online at www .NeeshaMeminger.com.

Lyn Miller-Lachmann is the former editor-in-chief of *Multi- Cultural Review* and the author of resources for educators and fiction for teens. Her young adult novel *Gringolandia* (Curbstone Press / Northwestern University Press 2009), about a teenage refugee from Chile coming to terms with his father's imprisonment and torture under the Pinochet dictatorship, was a 2010 ALA Best Book for Young Adults and received an Américas Award Honorable Mention from the Consortium of Latin American Studies Programs. Her most recent novel, *Rogue* (Penguin /Nancy Paulsen Books 2013), portrays an eighth grader with undiagnosed Asperger syndrome and an X-Men obsession, whose struggle to befriend another outcast after being expelled from school leads her to some difficult and dangerous choices. When she isn't writing, Lyn is the assistant host of a bilingual program of Latin American and Spanish music, poetry, and history on WRPI-FM and a part-time seventh grade teacher. She is a graduate of the Writing for Children & Young Adults program at Vermont College of Fine Arts and reviews children's and young adult books on social justice themes for *The Pirate Tree* (www.thepiratetree .com). Currently, she is working on a young adult novel and a middle grade novel. For more information, visit Lyn's website, www .lynmillerlachmann.com.

Jennifer A. Nielsen has been a rule breaker for her entire life. Her reckless indifference to social norms includes eating dessert before dinner, using a #1 pencil to answer test questions, and yes, she has been known to run with scissors (kid-safety scissors though—she's not a complete fool!). She currently lives in northern Utah with a husband, three children, and a dog that only obeys the rules if it smells a treat. She is the author of The Ascendance trilogy (Scholastic Paperbacks), The Underworld Chronicles series (Sourcebooks Jabberwocky), and is one of the authors with the Infinity Ring series (Scholastic Inc.). Learn more about her at www.jennielsen.com.

Mitali Perkins was born in India and immigrated to the States with her parents and two sisters when she was seven. Bengali-style, their names rhyme: Sonali means "gold," Rupali means "silver," and "Mitali" means "friendly." Mitali had to live up to her name because her family moved so much—she's lived in India, Ghana, Cameroon, England, New York, Mexico, California, Bangladesh, Thailand, and Massachusetts. Mitali studied political science at Stanford University and public policy at UC Berkeley before deciding to try and change the world by writing stories for young readers. Now she's settled in Newton, a town just outside of Boston, where she writes full-time. Visit her on the web at www.mitaliperkins.com.

Matthew Quick (aka Q) is the author of *The Silver Linings Playbook* (Sarah Crichton Books / Farrar, Straus & Giroux 2008) and three young adult novels, *Sorta Like a Rock Star, Boy21,* and *Forgive Me, Leonard Peacock* (Little, Brown). His work has received many honors—including a PEN/Hemingway Award Honorable Mention—been translated into several languages, and called "beautiful ... first-rate" by the *New York Times Book Review*. The Weinstein Company and David O. Russell have adapted *The Silver Linings Playbook* into a feature film starring Robert De Niro, Bradley Cooper, and Jennifer Lawrence. Matthew lives in Massachusetts with his wife, novelist Alicia Bessette. Visit him here: www.matthewquickwriter.com.

Margo Rabb is the author of *Cures for Heartbreak* (Delacorte 2008), which won the Teddy Children's Book Award and was named one of the best YA books of the year by *Kirkus* and *Booklist*. Her fiction and essays have been published in the *New York Times*, the *Atlantic, Zoetrope, Seventeen, One Story, Best New American Voices*, and elsewhere, and have been broadcast on National Public Radio. She received grand prize in the *Zoetrope* fiction contest, first prize in the *Atlantic* fiction contest, first prize in the *American Fiction* contest, and won a PEN Syndicated Fiction Award. Her new novel will be published by Random House in 2014.

Jennifer Reynolds has written articles on gender and self-image for *Mutuality* and researches human trafficking with the aim of developing strategies to further public awareness and protection for trafficking victims. Writing is one of her ultimate passions, and she absolutely loves working on stories for young adults, including her current project: a novel about the power of intergenerational relationships. Previously, she volunteered as an AmeriCorps Vista through Massachusetts Campus Compact, working as the Civic Engagement Coordinator at Mount Ida College near Boston. She has a passion for breaking rules about gender roles, image, and injustice.

Olugbemisola Rhuday-Perkovich is the author of the middle grade novel *8th Grade Superzero*, from Arthur A. Levine / Scholastic. She has 10-plus years in literacy education and youth development work with children, adults, and families, and looks forward to sharing the great power of the written word for many more. She contributed to various teen fanzines and developed educational materials geared to adolescents for organizations including Girls, Inc., React.com, and Sunburst Communications. Olugbemisola is a member of the Society of Children's Book Writers and Illustrators (SCBWI), PEN, and was twice-awarded an Echoing Green Fellowship for literacy and creative arts work with teen girls. Reading and writing have always been Olugbemisola's paths to meaning-making: "I spent a number of my younger years traveling to and living in different places. I attended public, private, 'international,' and religious schools. Each move brought with it opportunities and challenges around identity—experiences that have a great impact on my writing and work with and for young people." She holds a master's degree in education, and a certificate in the teaching of writing from the Teachers College Reading and Writing Project at Columbia University.

Pat Schmatz is the author of four novels for teens. Her early books were recognized by the Wisconsin Library Association, the Council for Wisconsin Writers, and Bank Street College of Education. Her most recent book, *Bluefish,* won the PEN / Phyllis Naylor Working Writer Fellowship while still a work in progress. It was published by Candlewick Press in 2011, and awarded Bank Street College of Education's 2012 Josette Frank Award for fiction and the SCBWI Crystal Kite Award for the Midwest. It is a Junior Library Guild Selection, an ALA Notable Children's Book, and winner of the Wisconsin Library Association's Elizabeth Burr / Worzalla Award. Pat grew up in rural Wisconsin. After adventures and stopovers in Michigan, California, Japan, and Minnesota, she is back in the Wisconsin woods, always working on another book.

Gary D. Schmidt writes for middle grade and young adult readers. His *Lizzie Bright and the Buckminster Boy* (Laurel Leaf 2008) won Newbery and Printz honors; his *The Wednesday Wars* (Clarion 2007) won another Newbery Honor; and his *Okay for Now* (Clarion 2011) won a Children's Choice Book Award and was a National Book Award finalist. He teaches in the English department of Calvin College and in the MFA in Writing for Children and Young Adults Program at Hamline University.

Lisa Schroeder is the author of many books for kids and teens, including young adult novels *Falling for You* (Simon Pulse 2013) and *The Day Before* (Simon Pulse 2011), and middle grade novels *It's Raining Cupcakes* (Aladdin 2010), *Sprinkles and Secrets*

(Aladdin 2011), and *Frosting and Friendship* (Aladdin 2013). When she's not writing, she enjoys walking the dog and baking sweet treats, though not at the same time. She lives in Oregon with her husband and two sons. You can find her on the web at www .lisaschroederbooks.com.

Tamara Ellis Smith is a writer who focuses on middle grade fiction and picture books. She is a graduate of the MFA program in writing for children and young adults at Vermont College of Fine Arts and is represented by Erin Murphy of Erin Murphy Literary Agency. You can learn more about her at www.tamaraellissmith .com and at Kissing the Earth, where she keeps a blog with writer Sharry Wright about the exploration of landscape and literature. Tamara makes her home in Richmond, Vermont. And for more information about Nate, his art, and his amazing Kanuwodi Art Retreat, which he created to mentor and guide Maine's youth to become more peaceful, responsible adults that give back to their communities and help their neighbors, please visit his websites at www.deveaugallery.com and www.kanuwodi.org.

Born in Poland and raised in the United States, **Anna Staniszew-ski** grew up loving stories in both Polish and English. She was named the 2006–7 Writer-in-Residence at the Boston Public Library and a winner of the 2009 PEN New England Susan P. Bloom Children's Book Discovery Award. Currently, Anna lives outside of Boston with her husband and their adopted black Labrador, Emma. When she's not writing, Anna spends her time teaching, reading, and challenging unicorns to games of hopscotch. She is the author of *My Very UnFairy Tale Life* and its sequel, *My Epic Fairy Tale Fail* (Sourcebooks Jabberwocky). Anna's first picture book, *Dogosaurus Rex,* is forthcoming from Henry Holt in Spring 2014. Visit her at www.annastan.com.

Francisco X. Stork is the award-winning author of five novels for young adults, including *Marcelo in the Real World* (Arthur A.

Levine Books 2009), *Irises* (Arthur A. Levine Books 2012), and *The Last Summer of the Death Warriors* (Arthur A. Levine Books 2010). He works as an attorney in Boston involved with helping to create affordable housing, and he is a graduate of Harvard University and Columbia Law School.

Carol Lynch Williams is the author of more than 20 books for middle grade and young adult readers. She's written nonfiction, historical fiction, and contemporary novels garnering many awards including ALA Quick Pick, ALA Best Fiction for Young Adults, PEN Award nominee, Children's Literature Choice List, "Honorable Mention" for Newton Books Best Books of the Year, IRA Teachers' Choice book, Selected Book for the Social Studies, Top Ten Romance Book for Booklist, Top Ten Barnes and Noble Book, Book for the Teen-Age List New York Public Library List, PEN/Phyllis Naylor Working Writer Fellowship, Scholastic Book Pick for Humor, and Audie Winner. She has an MFA in Writing for Children and Young Adults from Vermont College, shares a blog with the amazing Ann Dee Ellis (throwingupwords.wordpress.com) and teaches creative writing at Brigham Young University. She runs the annual weeklong writing conference Writing and Illustrating for Young Readers (www.wifyr.com). Her biggest achievement? Carol is most proud of her five daughters: Elise, Laura, Kyra, Caitlynne, and Carolina.

Brian Yansky has published three novels for young adults and several stories for adults. His latest novel is titled *Alien Invasion and Other Inconveniences* (Candlewick Press 2000). A sequel to that novel comes out in fall 2013 and another novel, *Utopia, Iowa*, will be published in 2014.

Sara Zarr is the acclaimed author of four novels for young adults. She is a National Book Award finalist and a two-time winner of the Utah Book Award. Her short fiction and essays have appeared in *Image, Hunger Mountain* online, and *Response*. She's also a regular contributor to *Image*'s Good Letters blog on faith, life, and culture. She lives in Salt Lake City, Utah, with her husband, and online at www.sarazarr.com.

Jennifer Ziegler is an author, speaker, blogger, mother, spicy food lover, caffeine addict, and champion doer-of-nothing. Her teen years were mainly spent trying to replicate the hairstyles of famous female pop figures (unsuccessfully), doodling designs for future tattoos (that she still hasn't gotten), memorizing dialogue from Bugs Bunny cartoons and Monty Python movies (which she can still quote), as well as reading, writing, and dreaming. Later she received degrees in English and journalism from the University of Texas at Austin and taught middle school language arts. She now writes novels for young adults. Each of her books, which include *How Not to Be Popular* (Delacorte 2008), *Alpha Dog* (Delacorte 2006), and *Sass & Serendipity* (Delacorte 2011), show how breaking tiny rules can lead to big discoveries. Jennifer lives in Austin, Texas, where, in addition to writing, she talks about her experiences at schools, libraries, conferences, and book festivals. She credits her wonderfully patient family and the vibrant Austin writing scene for keeping her happy and inspired.

ABOUT THE EDITOR

Luke Reynolds has taught seventh through twelfth grade English in public schools in Connecticut and Massachusetts. In addition to wearing basketball shorts in the winter, refusing to trim his nose hairs, and pretending to be an ogre when he walks down grocery store aisles, Luke deeply believes in the power of breaking lots of other rules—especially those involved in the fight for a more just, loving world. Luke is the author of *A Call to Creativity: Writing, Reading, and Inspiring Students in an Age of Standardization* (Teachers College Press 2012) and *Keep Calm and Query On: Notes on Writing (and Living) with Hope* (Divertir 2012); and he is coeditor of *Burned In: Fueling the Fire to Teach* (Teachers College Press 2011) and *Dedicated to the People of Darfur: Writings on Fear, Risk, and Hope* (Rutgers University Press 2009). His writing is represented by the marvelous Ammi-Joan Paquette of the Erin Murphy Literary Agency. Luke lives in Massachusetts.